Multinationals
and
Canada–United States
Free Trade

**CRITICAL ISSUES FACING
THE MULTINATIONAL ENTERPRISE**

Brian Toyne, Series Editor

Multinationals and
Canada–United States Free Trade
by Alan M. Rugman

International Business
and Governments: Issues
and Institutions
*by Jack N. Behrman
and Robert E. Grosse*

Multinationals
and
Canada–United States
Free Trade

by Alan M. Rugman

University of South Carolina Press

Copyright © University of South Carolina 1990

Published in Columbia, South Carolina, by the
University of South Carolina Press

First Edition

Manufactured in the United States of America

Library of Congress Cataloging-in-Publication Data

Rugman, Alan M.
    Multinationals and Canada-United States free trade / by Alan M.
Rugman. — 1st ed.
        p.   cm. — (Critical issues facing the multinational
enterprise)
    Includes bibliographical references.
    ISBN 0-87249-625-2
    1. United States—Foreign economic relations—Canada.   2. Canada—
Foreign economic relations—United States.   3. United States—
Commerce—Canada.   4. Canada—Commerce—United States.
5. International business enterprises—Canada.   6. International
business enterprises—United States.   7. Investments, American—
Canada.   8. Investments, Canadian—United States.   I. Title.
II. Series.
HF1456.5.C2R84   1989   Ll6747
382.0971073—dc20   89-24814
                                                                                            CIP

Contents

Contents

Illustrations

Series Editor's Preface

The purpose of this series is to explore the multifaceted relationship of multinational enterprises (MNEs) with their global environment. Essentially, each book in the series is written by an expert, and addresses a single issue of recognizable concern to MNEs. Thus, the aim of each book is to draw together and present the views of the various groups interested in the issue in a way that presents constructive suggestions for multinationals, irrespective of their nationality and inherent interests. Toward this end, each issue is placed in its historical setting and explored from the perspective of the MNEs, their home countries, and the host countries in which they operate—where they agree and where they disagree, and why. Of particular concern are the differences that have emerged, or are emerging, by region (even by country when necessary) and among multinationals from different parts of the world.

Thoughtful practitioners will find the series helpful in developing a better understanding of the organizations they work for, and interact or compete with. They will also gain a much better appreciation of the extent of the MNE's social, economic and political influence. Specifically, the series is designed to provide a "library" of the many views taken toward the multinational by the governments, labor organizations, and societies in which they operate or intend to operate, and the reasons for these differing views.

Educators will also find the series of value as a supplemental set of readers for topics in business administration, economics, international relations, and political science courses. Because of the scope of the series, and its historical perspective, students will eventually have access to an extensive and thorough analysis of the MNE, the role it plays, the influence it has on the global economic and political order, and thus the way it is viewed by other societal organizations.

The topic of *Multinationals and Canada-United States Free Trade* by Alan M. Rugman is both timely and important. Notwithstanding the considerable attention focused on Japan-United States trading relations in the media, the largest trading relationship in the world is between Canada and the United States. Thus, any change in this relationship will have political, social and economic consequences that reach well beyond the borders of these two countries. Importantly, the focus of Dr. Rugman's analysis is on the linkage between international trade and the international investment activities of MNEs as affected by potential changes in trading relations between two countries of disproportionate sizes. Consequently, its findings, partly because of the author's Canadian perspective, and partly because of the advent of Europe 1992, will be of interest to both scholars and practitioners.

Brian Toyne
Series Editor

Preface

This is a revised version of a study prepared for the Economic Council of Canada over the period of September 1986 to May 1987. This was a time when the prospects for bilateral free trade were the subject of seemingly endless debate in Canada and to a growing extent in the United States. As an indirect participant in the trade negotiations through my membership on the Government of Canada's International Trade Advisory Committee (ITAC), I feel that it is more important than usual to stress that this work is that of an independent scholar, and that it has not been sponsored by any government agency or private-sector corporation.

At the same time I wish to acknowledge a great debt to my private-sector colleagues on the ITAC and to several members of the federal and provincial bureaucracies involved in the formulation of trade policy, for providing me with realistic insights into the process of adjustment and investment that may result from proposals for bilateral and multilateral trade liberalization. I am also indebted to the chief executive officers and other senior managers involved in strategic planning, for their time and trouble in responding to the adjustment questionnaire reported in chapter 7.

My thinking on multinational enterprises has been greatly influenced by my former teachers and colleagues such as Harry G. Johnson, Herbert Grubel, Ray Vernon, Dick Caves, Charles Kindelberger, John Dunning, and Mark Casson. My understanding of U.S.-Canadian economic relations has been sharpened considerably by the advice and counsel of experts such as Ed Safarian, Don MacCharles, Murray Smith, Wendy Dobson, Dick Lipsey, Sandy Moroz, Bernie Wolf, Don Daly, Lorraine Eden, and other friends and colleagues too numerous to list.

I wish to thank members of the staff of the Economic Council of Canada for inviting me to prepare this study. In particular, I have enjoyed the penetrating criticisms and insights provided by the team assembled by Dr. Sunder Magun. In addition, I appreciate the constructive advice by the chairman, Judith Maxwell and the directors, Peter M. Cornell and William E. Alexander.

At the Dalhousie University Centre for International Business Studies remarkably good research assistance on the entire work was provided by Andrew Anderson. Invaluable help with chapter 6 was received from Visiting Research Fellow Dr. Alain Verbeke, who is the coauthor of this chapter. The immense burden of the word processing work was handled in a professional and speedy manner by the administrative secretary of the centre, Ms. Betty Evans. At the University of Toronto's Faculty of Management, research assistance was provided by Mark Warner and Ken Watson and secretarial help by Kay Rousseau. For advice on the publication of this book I thank series editor Brian Toyne.

None of the above named people bears any responsibility for the final product: that is mine alone.

A. M. R.

Multinationals
and
Canada–United States
Free Trade

Chapter 1

Free Trade and Foreign Direct Investment

THE UNITED STATES—CANADA
ECONOMIC RELATIONSHIP

The largest trading partner of the United States is not Japan—it is Canada. In fact, there is three times as much trade between the two North American countries as there is between the United States and Japan. About 25 percent of all U.S. exports go to Canada and nearly 80 percent of Canada's exports go to the United States. The largest trading relationship in the world takes place between Canada and the United States. In addition, these two countries account for the largest two-way flow of foreign direct investment in the world.

The significance of this Canada-United States foreign direct investment can be appreciated by consideration of the magnitude of bilateral investment compared to bilateral trade. The total value of Canada-United States trade (exports plus imports) for 1984 was about Cdn. $186 billion. In contrast, the total sales volume resulting from bilateral foreign direct investment (sales by U.S. subsidiaries in Canada plus sales by Canadian affiliates in the United States) was 60 percent greater, at nearly Cdn. $300 billion. Furthermore, the sales of the "billion dollar club," the 43 largest U.S. subsidiaries and Canadian multinationals, accounted for Cdn. $130 billion, or nearly half of the bilateral sales of all the multinationals.

Within the structure of today's globally integrated economy the close economic ties between Canada and the United States serve as a model to help us understand the complexities of international business. Both countries are now home and host nations for foreign direct investment. There are still major U.S. multinationals in Canada, but today there are also large Canadian-owned multinationals in the United States, such as Seagram, Northern Telecom,

1

Alcan, Noranda, and Abitibi-Price. The Reichmann brothers, from Toronto, are reported to own 8 percent of Manhattan, including the World Financial Center. The maturation of the Canadian economy and the recent development of Canada's own multinationals offer important lessons for the United States as it too becomes aware of the two-way flows of direct investment that dominate today's richest economies.

The political, social and cultural implications of this close economic relationship between Canada and the United States have been at the forefront of recent Canadian thinking. Largely at the behest of Canada, the world's most important bilateral trade agreement was negotiated over the 1986–1987 period. On 2 January 1988, President Ronald Reagan and Prime Minister Brian Mulroney signed the Canada-U.S. Free Trade Agreement. Subsequently ratified by the U.S. Congress and Canadian Parliament the Agreement became effective on 1 January 1989. The treaty was the catalyst for path-breaking economic and managerial studies about the nature of two-way trade and investment.

This study is an attempt, from the perspective of a Canadian academic, to capture some of these issues, especially the nature of foreign direct investment by both home and host country multinationals.

CANADIAN TRADE AND DIRECT INVESTMENT

The focus of this study is the linkage between international trade and the international investment activities of multinational enterprises involved in the Canadian economy. Such foreign direct investment is now a major world phenomenon. Indeed, Stopford and Dunning (1983) estimate that there are now over 10,000 multinational enterprises in the world, but the largest 500 of these account for 80 percent of all foreign direct investment. In 1981 the total sales of these 500 multinationals amounted to U.S. $2,700 billion, which is over half the value of the world's international exchange. Of these 500 multinational enterprises, about half (242) come from the United States, 172 from Europe, 62 from Japan, and 18 from Canada. A multinational enterprise is defined as an organization that engages in the production and distribution of goods and services in two or more nations. For a discussion of this and alternative definitions see Rugman (1981), chapter 1.

Canada is especially open to the influence of multinational enterprises; indeed Canada is best viewed in economic terms as a small (on a world scale), open, trading economy, where today the role of multinational enterprises at least matches that of trade itself. This implies that Canadian trade policy is also an investment policy. Put another way, the successful implementation of any substantial changes in trading relationships will require appropriate responses from the multinationals that are an integral part of Canada's economy. We need to know, as changes occur in the political and legal environment affecting Canada's trading relationships, how will direct investment react? In particular, how are the potential adjustment costs of trade liberalization affected by the presence in Canada of both foreign-owned multinational enterprises, and today, an increasing number of Canadian-owned multinationals operating in the United States and other nations?

Due to its current policy relevance primary attention in this book will be directed towards analysis of the adjustment impact of bilateral trade liberalization. However, considered indirectly will be the investment implications of trade liberalization within the eighth round of the General Agreement on Tariffs and Trade (GATT) as established in Uruguay in September 1986. The primary focus leads to research on two dimensions of foreign direct investment: first, the role of U.S. multinational enterprises in Canada and second, the newer presence of Canadian multinationals in the United States. Together the intra-firm sales of these two sets of multinationals have been estimated to account for nearly 70 percent of all bilateral trade in manufactured products (MacCharles 1985a).

From this it can be deduced that the adjustment costs of bilateral trade liberalization will be borne largely by such multinational enterprises. Indeed, since about 200 multinationals account for the great bulk of bilateral exchange, the successful implementation of the Canada-U.S. free trade agreement rests largely upon the shoulders of the strategic planning teams of these firms. It is also known that it is in the self-interest of these firms to minimize disruption of their business activities as they restructure and otherwise effect transitions to new trading rules. Therefore, to an extent, the social burden of adjustment is absorbed by these multinational enterprises as they act in their private interests. This implies that the so-called adjustment costs (especially of labour) may be less than forecast in economic models that neglect direct investment and do not capture the discretionary nature of strategic planning and management decision making.

Another objective of this book is to supplement and offer a more realistic alternative to the traditional economics based models of trade adjustment. This will be achieved by shifting the focus towards analysis of the actual multinational enterprises present in the adjustment process. This requires that data be presented identifying relevant trade and investment-related characteristics of the largest U.S. subsidiaries in Canada and the largest Canadian multinationals in the United States. These data also need to be related to the literature on intra-industry trade, derived especially from the experience of the European Economic Community (EEC), where cross-investment by multinationals abounds.

Finally, data on the degree and growth of bilateral intra-industry trade and production need to be gathered and used to help evaluate the manner in which trade liberalization will alter the activities of multinational enterprises. This leads to a type of social benefit cost analysis in which the employment-related effects of trade liberalization can be studied by analysis of the structure and patterns of intra-firm trade and investment, and the manner in which these may be altered by the managers of the multinational enterprises.

On a theoretical plane, the process of adjustment within the multinational enterprises needs to be examined from the viewpoint of management theory, especially strategic planning, as taught in business schools. In particular, relevant aspects of the transaction cost approach to the explanation of foreign direct investment help to explain why multinationals need to internalize control over intermediate products such as proprietary "knowhow."

Rugman (1981) and Caves (1982) offer summaries of the modern literature on the theory of the multinational enterprise; this work is now well known as internalization theory. An appreciation of internalization theory leads to a richer understanding of the managerial imperatives involved in an analysis of the costs of adjustment to a new trade regime. This combination of empirical and theoretical research on the multinational enterprise adds new dimensions to analysis of trade policy, dimensions that are missing from economics-based models of adjustment that cannot handle factors such as intra-industry trade and the subtleties of multinational behavior.

The plan of the book is as follows. The first half deals with aggregate data on foreign direct investment. The remainder of this first chapter presents basic data on the extent of U.S. direct investment in Canada and of Canadian direct investment in the United States. An appendix relates the history of Canada-United States trade and investment relations. Chapter 2 surveys the literature on direct investment, in particular the extent to which trade and investment are substitutes or complements. Chapter 3 presents for the first time a symmetrical analysis of the two sets of multinationals active in bilateral trade investment. Within the focus of a discussion of intra-firm trade, data are developed on the exports of U.S. subsidiaries and contrasted with their imports. The same is done for Canadian affiliates in the United States. Chapter 4 analyzes these data to determine the net benefits to Canada of this direct investment activity. An appendix provides more detail on the process through which the benefits of intra-industry trade accrue to Canada.

In the remainder of the study disaggregated data are used. Chapter 5 identifies the largest multinationals with sales of $1 billion or more. Also discussed is the extent of their international operations and their performance. This chapter provides the background for the discussion to follow on the strategic management decisions faced by these firms as a result of trade liberalization. Chapter 6 complements chapter 2 by undertaking a systematic theoretical discussion of the strategic management factors involved in firm adjustment to trade liberalization. Chapter 7 reports the nature and results of a questionnaire sent to the largest multinationals. The manner in which they will adjust to trade liberalization is revealed.

**RECENT TRENDS OF U.S. FOREIGN
DIRECT INVESTMENT IN CANADA**

From a Canadian perspective the United States is still the major source of foreign direct investment. For many years now nearly 80 percent of all foreign direct investment in Canada has come from the United States. The industrial strength of the United States is today being challenged by Japanese and other Asian competitors, by a revitalized Western Europe, and by state-owned enterprises from third world countries. The large U.S. current account deficit over the last five years (Cdn. $160 billion for 1985 alone) has been financed by growing capital account deficits, indicating net inflows of financial and foreign direct investment. Yet the United States is still an engine for world trade and investment. As well as playing host to inflows of foreign direct investment it is still the world's largest home country for the export of direct investment.

This section examines the size and signficance of U.S. foreign direct investment in Canada, the sectoral composition of such U.S. direct investment, and recent trends. Finally, the nature of a new phenomenon is explored— the outflows of Canadian direct investment to the United States. This has very important implications for U.S. and Canadian trade and investment policy.

Size of United States Direct Investment

Table 1.1 reports data on the stock of U.S. foreign direct investment in Canada for the last twelve years. The stock during this period has increased (in absolute terms) from 32 to 75 billion dollars. Such additions to the stock of foreign direct investment include the net flows plus the reinvested earning of U.S. subsidiaries in Canada. The average rate of increase in the U.S. stock has been over 8 percent per annum, with considerable variation, especially over the last five years.

During the recession of 1982, worsened by the tightened administration of the Foreign Investment Review Act (FIRA)

Table 1.1

United States Stocks of Foreign Direct
Investment in Canada
1976–1985

	Canada	Percent Growth
	(millions C$)	%
1976	31,917	7.59
1977	34,720	8.78
1978	38,352	10.46
1979	42,775	11.53
1980	48,686	13.82
1981	52,123	7.06
1982	52,640	0.99
1983	56,390	7.12
1984	62,359	10.59
1985	63,375	1.63
1986	67,700	6.82
1987*	75,200	11.08
Average Annual Percent Growth (1976–1987)		8.12

Note: *As of Dec. 31, 1987.

Sources: Canada, Statistics Canada, Canada's *International Investment Position: 1981 to 1984* (Ottawa: Supply and Services Canada, Catalogue 67–202, May 1986): Table 19 for 1975–1984, pp. 58–59.

Data for 1985–1987 supplied by the International Investment Position of the International and Financial Economics Division of Statistic Canada.

and the implementation of the National Energy Program (Rugman 1983b), there was an increase of under 1 percent in the U.S. stock of foreign direct investment in Canada. In fact at that time there were large net outflows of direct investment (of over Cdn. $11 billion in 1981, see Rugman [1987], chapter 1 and the technical appendix). Only the large amount of retained earnings kept the stock growing.

Dominance of United States Direct Investment

Table 1.2 indicates that Americans owned 76.3 percent of the stock of foreign direct investment in Canada in 1984. The slight decline from the historical norm of 80 percent of U.S. ownership is due to a recent doubling of the Japanese

Table 1.2

Area of Ownership of Foreign Direct Investment in Canada
(Stock at Year End, millions C$)

	1984	%	1980	%
North America				
United States	62,359	76.3	48,686	79.0
Other	1,141	1.4	939	1.5
	63,500	77.7	49,625	80.5
South and Central America	248	0.3	103	0.2
	248	0.3	103	0.2
Europe				
United Kingdom	7,342	9.0	5,333	8.7
EEC (Excluding U.K)	5,983	7.3	4,303	7.0
Other Europe	1,997	2.4	1,350	2.2
	15,322	18.7	10,986	17.9
Africa	253	0.3	138	0.2
	253	0.3	138	0.2
Asia				
Japan	1,752	2.1	605	1.0
Other Asia	464	0.6	107	0.2
	2,216	2.7	712	1.2
Australia	237	0.3	80	0.1
	237	0.3	80	0.1
Total	81,776	100.0	61,644	100.1

Source: Canada, Statistics Canada, *Canada's International Investment Position 1981 to 1984,* (Ottawa: Supply and Services Canada, Catalogue 67–202, May 1986): Table 19 for 1980 and 1984, p. 58.

stake in Canada (now at 2.1 percent) and a slight increase
in European investment, which is now at 18.7 percent of the
total. (Of this, British investment is today only 9 percent of
the total stock.)

Sectoral Composition of Direct Investment

Table 1.3 is the first of two dealing with industry and
sectoral aspects of foreign direct investment in Canada. Table 1.3 confirms the dominance of the United States as the

Table 1.3

Country Share of Foreign Direct Investment
in Canada, by Sector
1982 (millions C$)

Industry Group	U.S.	%[1]	U.K.	%[1]	Other	%[1]	Total
Manufacturing:							
Vegetable Products	2,754	75.60	460	12.63	429	11.78	3,643
Animal Products	444	80.00	9	1.62	102	18.38	555
Textiles	492	80.39	75	12.35	45	7.35	612
Wood and Paper Products	2,825	77.72	392	10.78	418	11.50	3,635
Iron and Products	7,863	92.93	330	3.90	268	3.17	8,461
Non-Ferrous Metals	2,470	85.14	99	3.41	332	11.44	2,901
Non-Metallic Metals	797	83.81	60	6.31	94	9.88	951
Chemical and Allied Products	4,523	86.05	463	8.81	270	5.14	5,256
Other Manufacturing	657	94.94	8	1.16	27	3.90	692
Sub-Total	22,825	85.47	1,896	7.10	1,985	7.43	26,706
Petroleum and Natural Gas	14,300	77.16	1,196	6.45	3,037	16.39	18,533
Mining and Smelting	2,513	63.32	421	10.61	1,035	26.08	3,969
Utilities	601	93.91	11	1.72	28	4.38	640
Merchandising	3,770	72.28	594	11.39	852	16.33	5,216
Financial	6,440	58.71	2,022	18.43	2,507	22.86	10,969
Other	2,191	78.17	204	7.28	408	14.56	2,803
Sub-Total	29,815	70.77	4,448	10.56	7,867	18.67	42,130
Total	52,640	76.47	6,344	9.22	9,852	14.31	68,836

Note: [1] of total F.D.I. in Canada.

Source: Canada. Statistics Canada. Canada's International Investment Position: 1981 to 1984 (Ottawa: Supply and Services Canada. Catalogue 67–202. May 1986): Table 18. pp. 54–57

leading foreign direct investor in Canada, across all the major sectors. For 1982 (the latest year of published data) the United States accounted for 85 percent of all of the stock of direct investment in manufacturing and 70 percent in all other sectors. At that time the United States held 77 percent of the stock of foreign direct investment in Canada's petroleum and natural gas sector. Yet since the introduction of the National Energy Program the proportion of *Canadian* ownership in the petroleum sector has increased to nearly 50 percent—a phenomenon not captured with these data.

Trends in the United States Sectoral Composition

Table 1.4 contains data on the sectoral composition of U.S. foreign direct investment in Canada (the first column of table 1.3). Manufacturing accounts for 43 percent of the U.S. total, petroleum and natural gas for 27 percent, and financial for 12 percent. Within manufacturing the biggest growth between 1978 and 1982 occurred in chemical products; the slowest growth in wood and paper products, textiles, and non-ferrous metals. Over this period there was actually a decline in the U.S. stock of direct investment in mining and smelting. Over the same period the fastest growth industry for U.S. foreign direct investment was finance at 74 percent.

Two-Way Direct Investment

Today the United States is not only a major direct investor in Canada, but also a major host country for foreign direct investment, including Canadian. The dramatic nature of this reversal, under which Canada has become a net exporter of foreign direct investment (mainly to the United States) is illustrated by data in table 1.5.

Table 1.5, column 2, reports the data on U.S. direct investment in Canada (the same data as in table 1.1, but now including the additional year of 1975). Column 1 of table 1.5 adds the data for Canadian direct investment in the United States. There has been an astonishing sevenfold increase in such Canadian foreign direct investment between 1975 and 1985. The average annual rate of increase has been over 20 percent.

Table 1.4

Sectoral Breakdown of the Stock of U.S. Foreign Direct Investment in Canada
1978 and 1982
(millions C$)

Industry Group	1982	%	1978	%	Change From 1978 to 1982 %
Manufacturing:					
Vegetable Products	2,754	5.23	2,055	5.35	34.01
Animal Products	444	0.84	352	0.92	26.14
Textiles	492	0.93	431	1.12	14.15
Wood and Paper Products	2,825	5.37	2,604	6.79	8.49
Iron and Products	7,863	14.95	6,329	16.50	24.24
Non-Ferrous Metals	2,470	4.69	2,037	5.32	21.26
Non-Metallic Metals	797	1.51	571	1.49	39.58
Chemicals and Allied Products	4,523	8.59	2,797	7.29	61.71
Other Manufacturing	657	1.25	430	1.12	52.79
Sub-Total	22,825	43.36	17,606	45.90	29.64
Petroleum and Natural Gas	14,300	27.17	8,894	23.19	60.78
Mining and Smelting	2,513	4.78	3,167	8.27	(21.32)
Utilities	601	1.14	586	1.53	2.56
Merchandising	3,770	7.16	2,874	7.49	31.18
Financial	6,440	12.23	3,693	9.63	74.38
Other Enterprises	2,191	4.16	1,532	3.99	43.02
Sub-Total	29,815	56.64	20,746	54.10	43.71
Total	52,640	100.00	38,352	100.00	37.25

Source: Canada, Statistics Canada, Canada's International Investment Position: 1981 to 1984 (Ottawa: Supply and Services, Canada, Catalogue 67–202, May 1986): Table 18, pp. 54–55

Table 1.5

Bilateral Stocks of U.S. Foreign Direct Investment
in Canada and the United States,
1975–1985 (millions C$)

	Canadian FDI Position in the U.S.	U.S. FDI Position in Canada	Net Position [(1)–(2)]	(1)/(2)
1975	5,559	29,666	–24,107	18.7
1976	6,092	31,917	–25,825	19.1
1977	7,116	34,720	–27,604	20.5
1978	8,965	38,352	–29,387	23.4
1979	12,063	42,775	–30,708	28.4
1980	16,386	48,686	–32,298	33.7
1981	21,831	52,123	–30,292	41.9
1982	23,137	52,640	–29,503	44.0
1983	25,528	56,390	–30,862	45.3
1984	29,932	62,359	–32,427	48.0
1985	35,474	63,375	–27,901	56.0
1986	39,800	67,700	–27,000	58.8
1987	43,300*	75,200	–31,900	57.6
Average Rate of Increase 1975– 1985	19.09%	8.12%		

*As of Dec. 31, 1987

Sources: Canada, Statistics Canada, Canada's International Investment Position: 1981–1984 (Ottawa: Supply and Services Canada, Catalogue 67–202, May 1986): Table 18, pp. 54–54 and Table 3, pp 30–31.

Data for 1985 suppled by the International Investment Position of the International and Financial Economics Division of Statistics Canada.

The result of the large outflows of Canadian foreign direct investment, coupled with the slower rate of increase of U.S. direct investment in Canada, is that the ratio of outward to inward investment has changed substantially. The last column of table 1.5 indicates that today Canada has the equivalent of 60 percent of the stock of U.S. direct investment in Canada, up from only 18.7 percent in 1975. If this trend continues, by the late 1990s Canada should have as much foreign direct investment in the United States as there is U.S. direct investment in Canada.

TWO-WAY FLOWS OF DIRECT INVESTMENT

From the data examined here it is clear that the single most important trend observed is the upsurge of Canadian direct investment in the United States. A recent study has explored the reasons for such outward investment and described the implications for Canadian and U.S. trade and investment policy (Rugman 1987). These reasons range from the attractiveness of the largest U.S. market to the presence of heightened U.S. administered protection, international risk diversification, and the mature pattern of the modern multinational exhibiting cross-investment and intra-industry trade. Yet the outflows of Canadian direct investment should not blind us to the fact that U.S. direct investment in Canada has still been growing.

What does it mean for Canada to have increases in both inward and outward direct investment? These data on direct investment reflect the increasing economic integration of the United States and Canada. The vehicle for such integration is the multinational enterprise. Canadians are well aware of the historical influence of U.S. multinationals on the Canadian economy. These firms are still here and Americans still own about half of Canada's manufacturing sector.

However, today we witness the presence of large Canadian-owned multinational enterprises operating successfully in the United States. Such multinationals as Canada's Alcan, Noranda, Seagram, Moore, Domtar, Bombardier, and others have secured an important stake in America. For a recent study on the corporate strategies and performance of Canada's 20 largest multinational enterprises, see Rugman and McIlveen (1985).

The growth of Canadian foreign direct investment in the United States is part of an upsurge from all the major trading partners of the United States. Indeed, Japanese and European direct investment has grown even faster than Canadian. The reason is that the United States market is the single largest and most diversified in the world. It is the magnet for direct investment and still the leading engine for world economic development.

The logic of geography favours Canada. Sitting next door
to the world's richest economy means that as firms on both
sides of the border continue to operate in one large integrated North American market there will be continuous U.S.
direct investment in Canada, across all sectors. There will
also be a corresponding rate of growth of Canadian direct
investment in the United States. These two-way flows of foreign direct investment reflect the realities of modern-day
business and strategic management. In a world of government regulation and decentralized administrative protection there is an increased rationale for organization of
exchange through multinational enterprises, rather than
via trade (Rugman 1981, Safarian 1985, and Rugman and
Anderson 1987).

As trade is liberalized between Canada and the United
States, either as part of a bilateral or multilateral process,
or both, it is likely that two-way direct investment will still
keep on expanding. Once multinational enterprises have
made strategic investment decisions it becomes difficult to
divest or move back towards other forms of involvement
such as trade, licensing, and joint ventures. Thus, in the future, Canada will become an even stronger part of an integrated global economic system activated by multinational
enterprises.

The real issue for policy makers to address is simple.
Are Canada and the United States in a position to secure
their appropriate shares of global direct investment? By
this I mean, for Canada, that it should first develop policies
to attract direct investment. If the Canadian government is
committed to the belief that more foreign investment is beneficial, it should extend the principle of national treatment
and abolish the residual screening powers of Investment
Canada. Both levels of government, federal and provincial,
should aggressively promote Canada's new investment potential. Second, Canada needs a policy environment that en-
courages the development of world-class Canadian-owned
multinationals. These firms are Canada's keys to the future.
Their success in the U.S. market and, ultimately, in the
global economy, is just as important to the welfare of Canadians as are sustained inflows of (mainly U.S.) direct
investment.

It has been shown here that foreign direct investment is a two-way street. For Canada, the United States accounts for some 80 percent of all inward direct investment and is also the leading host to Canadian outward investment. These investment flows are today largely determined by large multinational enterprises, Canadian as well as American. The role of governments in both nations should be to provide a more predictable and stable investment climate, so that multinational enterprises can continue to increase the prosperity of both Canadians and Americans.

A History of United States-Canada Trade and Investment Relations

To understand the relevance of this study of the role of multinationals in current U.S.-Canadian trade and investment policy it is helpful to consider the history of this bilateral relationship. For a more detailed account of these policies see Granatestein (1985), Whalley (1985), Lea (1963), and Rugman (1981). For some 150 years the issue of free trade has been an important issue in Canadian politics and U.S. economics. Due to the fact that the Canadian economy is only about one-tenth the size of the United States the free trade issue has never been as important in U.S. politics as it has been in Canadian politics.

In 1854 Governor General Lord Elgin of Canada traveled to Washington to negotiate a Reciprocity Treaty. Elgin had lobbied the southern U.S. Senators to support the treaty since they shared a common interest with the Canadians. By providing free trade between the two countries, the Canadian sovereignty would be protected as would the power of the southerners within the American Union.

The resulting Elgin-Marcy treaty provided for free trade in primary products such as fish, lumber, grain, and coal, and for reciprocal use of the Atlantic fisheries and St. Lawrence-Great Lakes waterways. With the reciprocal free trade about 55 percent of U.S. imports into the province of Canada entered duty free as did 90 percent of Canadian exports to the United States. The treaty lasted only until 1866, when the United States refused to renew the treaty. The United States disliked the tariffs imposed by Canada beginning in 1859 to protect its new manufacturing industry.

The loss of the ready access to the U.S. market helped lead to the eventual confederation of the six British North

---

*This appendix was prepared by Mark Warner, Research Assistant at the University of Toronto.

American provinces into the Dominion of Canada in 1867. Subsequently, the Canadian Minister of Finance traveled to Washington in 1869 to offer free or equal access to the Canadian fishery and entrý of certain manufactured goods, in return for free entry of Canadian natural resource products into the United States. The Americans were not interested. Again in 1871, when the British and Americans negotiated the Treaty of Washington to regulate the use of the inshore fishery and waterways, Prime Minister John A. MacDonald of Canada called for the renewal of the Elgin-Marcy treaty. The Americans again refused to negotiate.

In 1874 the Liberal government of Alexander Mackenzie sent an envoy to negotiate a sectoral treaty, with a tariff-free list of natural resources and a substantial number of manufactured goods. While President Grant seemed in favour, the treaty foundered in the Senate. Many U.S. Senators saw in the agreement an attempt to give England free trade through the back door, and this was at odds with the protectionist sentiment prevailing at the time in the United States.

CANADA'S NATIONAL POLICY AND THE RECIPROCITY DEBATE OF 1911

These U.S. rebuffs led to the introduction of the "National Policy" in 1879 by the Conservative Prime Minister John A. MacDonald. This policy provided a secure national market for protected Canadian manufactured goods, helped by a national transportation (railway) policy and active government support for westward settlement. In 1891, with MacDonald still in power, the Canadian government entered into secret discussions with the United States regarding reciprocity. When the negotiations failed the U.S. Secretary of State James G. Blaine stated that Canada had to choose between its historic British link and closer ties to the United States. By the 1890s the Americans were arguing for a customs union with a common external tariff. Canada was not willing or able to grant to the United States more favourable treatment than that accorded Great Britain and her colonies.

Again in 1896, another set of negotiations failed and Canada then introduced what have become known as the

Fielding tariffs, after the Liberal finance minister of the time. The Liberal government of Wilfred Laurier simply strengthened the old "National Policy." However, they left the door open for the United States to negotiate on a reciprocal basis. The Fielding tariffs allowed Canada to retaliate against the American Dingley tariffs without raising the general Canadian tariff level. At the same time Canada instituted a tariff preference system towards Great Britain, even though these concessions went unreciprocated.

One result of the Fielding tariff was the creation of the branch plant "tariff factories" which still rest at the heart of the Canadian debate about trade and investment links to the United States. In 1904, Fielding noted for the first time the success of the tariff in bringing U.S. manufacturing industry across the border. In fact in 1900 the U.S. share of all non-resident direct and portfolio investment was 14 percent and that of Britain was 85 percent. As table A1.1 demonstrates, by 1916 the U.S. share had risen to 30 percent while the British share had declined to 66 percent. So until the Great War, Canada was very much tied to the British empire and U.S. investment was not an issue, although foreign direct investment in general had increased due to protective tariffs.

In 1909 the United States imposed the Payne-Aldrich tariff on newsprint: this permitted the imposition of the maximum rate against countries that discriminated against the United States. In 1910 the United States claimed that some Canadian concessions made to France in 1906 constituted such discrimination and threatened to impose the maximum tariff. President Taft, however, sent a delegation to Ottawa to negotiate. He wanted an agreement before the election in order to placate U.S. newspaper publishers who wanted access to the cheaper Canadian product.

Finally, in 1911, Fielding and U.S. Secretary of State P. C. Knox reached an historic agreement in Washington. The agreement consisted of four schedules: Schedule A provided reciprocal trade for some goods; schedule B lowered duties identically on some goods; and schedules C and D dealt with specific goods from each country. It has been estimated that had the agreement succeeded, 50 percent of Canadian imports from the United States and 80 percent of

Table A1.1

Foreign Investment in Canada

Year	U.S. Total Investment All Foreign Investment	U.K. Total Investment All Foreign Investment	U.S. FDI Total Foreign Investment	U.S. FDI Total FDI
		Percent		
1900	14	85	–	–
1905	19	79	–	–
1910	19	77	–	–
1916	30	66	–	–
1922	50	47	–	–
1926	53	44	23	79
1933	61	36	26	82
1939	60	36	27	82
1945	70	25	33	85
1950	76	20	40	86
1955	76	18	48	84
1960	75	15	48	82
1965	79	12	48	79
1970	79	9	48	81
1975	77	8	43	79
1980	69	7	38	79
1985	56	7	28	76
1987	48	8	26	73

Note: Data prior to 1926 are estimates.

Source: Statistics Canada, *Canada's International Investment Position* 67–202: 1977, 1981–84, 1982–85. Data for 1987 obtained from statistics Canada, Balance of Payments Division.

U.S. imports from Canada would have been duty free. Taft secured Congressional approval with some difficulty. However, in Canada an election ensued, and the Conservative leader defeated the Laurier government on a platform of "No truck nor trade with the Yankees." The Canadian Manufacturers Association played a major role in support of protection and against bilateral free trade in the reciprocity debate of 1911.

The 1911 agreement was significant in many respects. It demonstrated the cyclical nature of demands on both sides of the border for free trade and the protectionism preferred by manufacturers on both sides of the border. The agreement emphasized a sectoral and gradual approach to trade liberalization.

INTER-WAR POLICIES

With the failure of the agreement, both countries were plunged into an era of protectionism. When the United States imposed its Fordney-McCumber tariffs in 1922, Canada followed with tariff increases. This pattern was to be repeated again in 1930 when the United States passed its Smoot-Hawley tariffs.

Even with the failure of the 1911 agreement, exogenous factors led Canada to closer economic ties with the United States. As Canada entered the war the Canadian government soaked up the market for bonds so that Canadian corporations turned to New York. Table 1 reports that in 1916 Americans held 30 percent of all foreign investment in Canada, but by 1920 this figure was up to 52 percent. Also in 1917 Canada and the United States signed an agreement that allowed Canada to make up for shortages in supplying the war effort. When in 1918 some U.S. industries complained that Canada was getting too great a share of the war production, Prime Minister Borden traveled to Washington to elicit the support of President Woodrow Wilson for the continuation of the war agreement.

Table A1.1 reports that in 1910 the U.S. share of total foreign investment (portfolio and direct) was 19 percent but by 1926 it had risen to 53 percent. Over the same period the British share declined from 77 percent to 44 percent. The U.S. share of foreign direct investment was 79 percent in 1926, and in successive years it began to make up an increasing proportion of all foreign investment (portfolio and direct). Clearly, the economies of the United States and Canada were moving towards greater integration.

THE CORDELL HULL AGREEMENT OF 1935

These economic forces towards greater economic integration were strengthened in 1934, when the new "Good Neighbor Policy" of President Franklin Roosevelt led to the passage of the Reciprocal Trade Agreements Act. With the support of Secretary of State Cordell Hull, who believed that

free trade and peace were synonymous, a new attempt at negotiating free trade was initiated. This resulted in the 1935
Canada-U.S. Bilateral Agreement in which each party
granted the other most-favoured nation status and tariff reductions below the intermediate rates for certain products.
This marked the first comprehensive trade agreement between the two countries since 1854, and in addition rolled
tariffs back to the pre-1922 Fordney-McCumber days. In
1938 this agreement was again strengthened. Canada removed some more preferences for Great Britain and the
Commonwealth, and some of the 1935 quotas were either
removed or the limits raised. Despite the position of the Canadian Manufacturers Association, public opinion favoured
free trade in the depression era as a means of gaining market access.

This new spirit continued until 1941 when President
Roosevelt and Prime Minister Mackenzie King signed the
Hyde Park agreement on Defense Production Sharing, in
Hyde Park, New York. By 1945 the U.S. share of FDI in Canada had risen to 85 percent while the United Kingdom
accounted for only 13 percent. This decline in British influence, combined with the internationalist mood on both
sides of the border, embodied in the participation in the formation of the GATT in 1947, led to another free trade initia-
tive in 1948.

POST-WAR POLICIES

In 1947, John Deutsch, Canadian economist and direc-
tor of the International Economics Division at the Department of Finance, began secret negotiations with Paul Nitze
of the U.S. State Department's Office of International Trade
Policy. The agreement envisaged by the two officials was
one of almost unrestricted free entry of goods across both
sides of the border after a phase-in period of five years for
adjustment. Under the scheme both parties would retain
the right to maintain their own third party tariffs, thus re-
moving one of the traditional Canadian obstacles. In practice, however, this factor had decreased in importance for
Canada. In addition, the agreement would estabish a principle of consultation in the sensitive area of agricultural marketing. In the end, Prime Minister Mackenzie King decided

Table A1.2

Bilateral Trade Shares
(Selected Years)

Year	U.S. Share of Canadian Exports	Canadian Share of U.S. Exports
	Percent	
1926	37.4	–
1945	32.6	–
1960	56.4	18.1
1970	64.8	22.5
1980	63.9	18.0
1987	76.3	23.7

Note: Canadian data for exports and imports were converted to U.S. dollars at year-end foreign exchange rates.

Sources: Statistics Canada, *Canada's International Investment Position* 67–202: 1977, 1981–84, 1982–85. Data for 1987 obtained from Statistics Canada, Balance of Payments Division.

Statistics Canada, *Summary of Canadian International Trade 1985*, Catalogue No. 65001. *Canadian International Investment Portfolio* Catalogue No. 67202, various issues. *Quarterly Estimates of the Canadian Balance of International Payments*, Catalogue No. 67001 various issues. *The Canadian Balance of International Payments*, Catalogue No. 67201, various issues.

International Financial Statistics, IMF Washington, D.C., various issues.

International Financial Statistics Yearbook, IMF Washington, D.C., various issues.

that the deal would be politically unacceptable and hence the deal was abandoned, despite the objections of the senior civil service mandarins such as Deutsch, Lester Pearson, and the important industry minister, C. D. Howe.

Despite the failure of this agreement the trend towards economic integration continued. Table A1.2 demonstrates that the U.S. share of Canadian exports rose from 37 percent in 1926 to 56 percent in 1960. Concern over this trend led John Diefenbaker, the Conservative prime minister, to try to diversify trade, especially to Britain. This policy, however, was ill fated, as in 1957 the EEC was formed under the Treaty of Rome. Although Britain did not join until 1973, it

was clear that the trend in Europe was to greater coopera-
tion. Secondly, by 1957 Canada had already benefited from
four rounds of GATT tariff reductions; these served to increase trade with the United States. In 1964, the Kennedy
round of the GATT began and by 1967 duties had been reduced by an average 35 percent. Canada and the United
States were moving towards even greater trade liberalization
and their two-way trade would continue to grow.

THE AUTO-PACT

This trend was symbolized in 1965 by the signing of the
Canada-U.S. Automobile Products Trade Agreement. By this
time transportation equipment was by far the largest manufacturing industry in Canada and was dominated by subsidiaries of the major U.S. automobile companies. This
sectoral trade agreement provided for duty free trade over
an array of products, subject to certain performance requirements. The U.S. Congress accepted the Auto Pact after
a major lobbying effort from President L. B. Johnson and
the Treasury and Commerce Departments.

While the arguments of Canadian economic nationalists
prior to 1935 focused on the nature of bilateral trade, from
1960 until the mid-1980s the debate switched to foreign investment. This Canadian concern led the Liberal government of Lester Pearson to appoint a Royal Commission to
determine the nature and extent of foreign investment in
Canada. This Gordon commission reported in 1962 and led
to the passage of the Corporations and Labour Unions Returns Act (CALURA). This Act required all corporations to
report detailed data on their sales, assets, and degree of foreign ownership.

ECONOMIC NATIONALISM IN CANADA

Despite the inceasing economic integration of the two
economies the political strength of the economic nationalists grew throughout the 1960s. By 1966, Canada's Liberal
government had issued Industry Minister Gillespie's non-
binding "Guidelines of Good Corporate Citizenship," and
had intervened to prevent the sale to foreign buyers of such
businesses as the Traders Group, Denison Mines, and
Home Oil. This trend was further reinforced when in 1968

the Watkins Report on the Foreign Ownership and Structure of Canadian Industry was published. This report argued that U.S. multinational corporations constrained the capacity for independent policy by the government of Canada. While granting the contributions of FDI to raising the Canadian standard of living, Watkins argued that such investment hindered indigenous Canadian economic growth. On the grounds of economic nationalism, Watkins called for the establishment of an agency to monitor operations and investments of foreign corporations and to consider the use of performance requirements for such firms.

In 1970 the Wahn Report of the Standing Committee on External Affairs and National Defence was published. While endorsing the Watkins report, Wahn went further, calling for at least 51 percent ownership of voting shares of all corporations over time. In addition the report called for a majority of Canadian citizens to sit on all corporate boards of directors. In calling for the establishment of an independent agency, the Wahn report suggested that such a body have both screening and decision-making powers.

Next, the Gray Report on Foreign Direct Investment in Canada was published in 1972. It proposed a process for screening of foreign investment that would rely on: cost-benefit analysis, case by case analysis, a bargaining process, policy guidance, and selection of the major transactions. In 1973, under the leadership of Pierre Trudeau, this long and arduous process culminated in the passage of the Foreign Investment Review Act, establishing FIRA as the review agency.

FIRA decisions on whether to permit or to block individual foreign investments were ultimately made by the Cabinet on the recommendation of the responsible minister. The threshold level for review was set initially at assets over Cdn. $250,000 and sales over Cdn. $3 million. While several factors were to be considered by the agency, the final test for acceptance or rejection of a case was determined by a test for "significant benefit" for Canada. In 1980, the Liberal government added performance reviews to the test of significant benefit. In 1982 the United States challenged the local procurement and export content features of the Act before a

GATT panel. The GATT panel found that the procurement requirements were unfair but allowed the export requirements to remain. Canada complied with these rulings by amending FIRA's guidelines.

Under the administration of FIRA the success rates varied depending on the cabinet minister in charge. In fact, under Herb Gray the acceptance rate for new acquisitions dropped to 73 percent in 1981 and 79 percent in 1982, see table A1.3 and Rugman (1983b). In the energy sector corresponding with the National Energy Policy (another interventionist policy aimed at gaining at least 51 percent Canadian control of the key energy sector) the acceptance rate fell to 18 percent in 1982, and in 1981 dropped to a low of 53 percent for new establishments. In addition, the NEP led to a capital outflow of slightly more than Cdn. $15 billion between 1980 and 1985.

TOWARDS FREE TRADE

In 1984 the newly elected Conservative government of Brian Mulroney changed FIRA to Investment Canada and in 1985 abandoned the National Energy Policy. Investment Canada is aimed at promoting an "open for business" investment policy. Henceforth, new establishments are no longer subject to review. In addition, investments are assessed for a "net benefit" to Canada, not a significant benefit. As table A1.3 demonstrates, acceptance rates under the new regime have inceased dramatically for both categories. In 1986 the success rate was 99 percent for acquisitions and 100 percent for new establishments.

In assessing these programs it should be noted that total foreign control of all non-financial corporations fell from 36 percent in 1975 to 29 percent in 1985 (see table A1.4). However, over the same period the U.S. share of all FDI in Canada has remained relatively constant at 76 percent. This decline in industry-wide foreign control is matched by specific sectoral declines between 1970 and 1985. For example, foreign control during this period fell from 56 to 49 percent in manufacturing alone, and from 99 to 57 percent in oil and gas. In keeping with the realization of the economic inefficiencies of these policies, in 1983 the Canadian Manu-

Table A1.3

FIRA Applications
Success Rates for Mines, Mineral Fuels, and
Incidental Services (M, MF, IS)

	M,MF,IS			Total all Industries			Success M,MF,IS	Success all Industry
	A.	D.	W.	A.	D.	W.	%	%
Acquisitions								
1986–87	28	–	1	642	–	10	96.6	98.5
1985–86	29	–	1	475	–	7	96.7	98.5
1984–85	23	–	2	464	4	26	92.0	93.9
1983–84	16	–	1	430	5	94	94.1	91.9
1982–83	17	5	4	469	13	65	65.4	90.5
1981–82	2	7	2	248	36	18	18.2	79.0
1980–81	5	5	3	215	36	39	38.5	73.4
1979–80	17	6	2	331	29	68	68.0	85.1
1978–79	19	–	2	296	26	91	90.5	87.8
New Establishments								
1986–87	5	–	–	313	–	–	100.0	100.0
1985–86	13	–	–	318	–	–	100.0	100.0
1984–85	12	1	1	474	6	27	85.7	93.5
1983–84	15	–	3	428	22	43	83.3	86.8
1982–83	15	–	1	455	47	59	93.8	81.1
1981–82	21	3	6	265	45	95	70.0	65.5
1980–81	8	1	6	233	27	33	53.3	79.5
1979–80	16	2	1	356	29	25	84.2	86.8
1978–79	15	–	4	280	18	24	78.9	87.0

Note: A = accepted applications
D = disallowed applications
W = withdrawn applications

Sources: Foreign Investment Review Agency, *Annual Reports* (various) 79–
80–84–85, especially Tables XI, XXI.

Investment Canada, *Annual Reports* 85–86, especially tables XIV,
XII. Data for 1986–87 obtained from Investment Canada.

facturers Association abandoned its century-old support
for tariffs and government regulations. Its calls for a bilateral Canada-U.S. free trade agreement were instrumental in
leading to the initiation of Prime Minister Mulroney in 1985.

Table A1.4

Foreign Control of Canadian Industry

	All Non-financial Corps		All Manufacturing		Petroleum + Coal	
	Total U.S.	Foreign	Total U.S.	Foreign	Total U.S.	Foreign
			Percentage			
1985	21.9	29.0	39.8	49.2	39.6	57.4
1984	22.8	29.7	40.8	50.4	54.4	71.0
1983	22.6	29.6	40.5	50.3	55.2	70.0
1982	22.0	29.2	38.7	49.5	53.5	77.6
1981	21.8	29.1	37.9	48.5	52.1	76.2
1980	24.1	31.7	40.5	51.2	57.3	82.1
1979	26.1	33.6	43.2	53.3	58.9	83.0
1978	26.2	33.5	45.0	55.5	65.2	88.2
1977	27.7	34.8	46.6	56.7	70.9	95.3
1976	27.4	34.5	46.0	56.0	69.0	96.0
1975	28.1	35.5	46.0	57.0	71.0	96.0
1974	27.9	36.7	46.0	57.0	72.0	96.0
1973	27.7	36.5	46.0	57.0	74.2	98.9
1972	28.1	36.5	47.1	57.2	77.5	99.1
1971	29.3	37.6	47.0	57.0	79.7	99.0
1970	28.4	37.0	46.0	56.0	77.0	98.7

Source: Statistics Canada 61–210 *Corporations and Labour Unions Returns Act,* Part I. 1985: Tables 1, 4; 1977–1984: Table 4; 1970–1976: Table 3.31.

CONCLUSIONS

To summarize, this section has traced how Canadian and U.S. attitudes towards free trade and direct investment have developed over the last 150 years. It would be wrong, however, to suggest that Canada alone has evolved a tradition of review for foreign investment. The Canadian approach embodied in FIRA and in Investment Canada is a formal procedure. Rugman (1987) demonstrated that the U.S. approach is a more informal procedure. In 1975, under executive order, the Committee on Foreign Investment in the United States (CFIUS) was established. This body was given the authority to review and to coordinate the implementation of U.S. policies towards inward direct investment.

Up until now CFIUS has concentrated on investments where "national interest" implications were of concern. However, as concerns about inward direct investment proliferate in the United States, the powers of such an agency could easily be expanded.

This latter issue takes on added significance in light of the increasing trend towards Canadian direct investment in the United States (Rugman 1986). Between 1975 and 1980 such Canadian investment has been growing at three times the rate of similar U.S. investment in Canada. By the late 1990s Candians will have as much direct investment in the United States as Americans have in Canada.

It has been demonstrated here that the Canadian-U.S. debate about free trade is not a recent development in the bilateral relations of both countries. It is clear that there is a long-term march towards closer trade and investment patterns. It is perhaps worth concluding this chapter with the reminder that Lord Elgin, in negotiating the first Reciprocity Treaty of 1854, convinced his U.S. counterparts that such fraternal economic ties were the surest way of securing both the economic well-being and political independence of both peoples. This is still true today and the recent Canada-U.S. free trade agreement offers an opportunity to proceed with mutually beneficial trade and investment policies.

Chapter 2

Trade Liberalization, Adjustment, and International Investment

In this chapter, analysis will focus upon foreign direct investment rather than portfolio (financial) investment since only direct investment involves control and is affected by major structural changes in the trading environment. Portfolio investment flows are broadly determined by the U.S.-Canadian interest rate differential and related monetary variables, whereas direct investment is dependent upon factors affecting the relative profitability of actual operations in the United States and Canada (Rugman 1980b, chapters 1, 2, and 11).

In terms of bilateral and multilateral trade liberalization there are three major areas where the linkages of trade and direct investment need to be considered:

1. The impact of trade liberalization on inward direct investment, especially the strategic responses of U.S.-owned multinationals in Canada to a new trading environment.

2. The effect of trade liberalization upon Canadian direct investment in the United States, and the responses of Canadian multinational enterprises (especially if U.S. non-tariff barriers to trade in the form of contingent protection are removed).

3. The nature of the adjustment process under new trade agreements when it is recognized that currently some 70 percent of U.S.-Canadian merchandise trade is intra-firm and that some 200 to 300 large U.S. and Canadian-owned multinational enterprises account for most of such internal transactions between parent and subsidiaries (for evidence see chapters 3 and 6).

Such multinationals are used to scan environmental factors (such as changes in trade policy) and they incorporate this information into their strategic planning decisions. To some extent this raises the possibility that economist's models of the adjustment costs of freer trade, which fre-

quently ignore intra-firm trade, may overestimate adjustment costs which, to a large degree, are borne by individual
multinationals.

Each of these three areas will be considered in detail in
this study. Before doing so, a few general principles will be
outlined. Analysis of both of the first two issues, dealing
with inward and outward direct investment, to an extent
hinges upon the question of whether direct investment and
trade are regarded as substitutes or complements.

TRADE AND DIRECT INVESTMENT: SUBSTITUTES OR COMPLEMENTS?

Some people tend to think of direct investment as a substitute for trade. For example, it is well known that much of
the major U.S. foreign direct investment into Canada was
motivated by the need to jump the Canadian tariffs first imposed in 1879 to protect Canadian industry. Instead, Canada secured a large degree of foreign ownership of its
industry (Rugman 1980b) and inefficiently sized plants
(Baldwin and Gorecki 1985). Recently, economists such as
Safarian (1985) and Burgess (1985, 1986) have argued that
with liberalized trade there will be an expansion of both
trade and investment. Lipsey (1986) argues that this is pre-
cisely what occurred with the formation of the EEC since
direct investment expanded in a complementary manner
with trade.

This argument that trade and investment are really complements (not substitutes) and that the relationship between them need not have negative effects on employment
is now examined in three ways. First, a simple example is
given. Second, a more technical discussion based on the literature of the modern theory of the multinational enterprise is developed. Finally, work by Safarian and Burgess in
this vein is reported.

From the viewpoint of the Canadian manager of either a
small or large firm already engaged in exporting to the
United States, the current escalation of U.S. "contingent
protection" is a type of non-tariff barrier to trade (Rugman
and Anderson 1987). This presents an incentive to switch
from exporting to foreign direct investment, an internal
managerial decision that will depend upon an evaluation of
the costs and benefits of such a switch of modality.

The costs of foreign direct investment, defined as production and distribution in a foreign nation (thus making the firm into a multinational enterprise), include the political and environmental risks of operating in a different nation. In general, Canadian firms experience lower entry barriers when starting up in the United States than in a less familiar nation such as Japan. Location acts as a major factor in reducing information costs and other uncertainties about subsidiary production in the United States, especially for the larger Canadian firms.

The reverse argument holds for U.S. foreign direct investment in Canada. The experience of foreign ownership is so familiar to Canadians that in this study a focus can be put, whenever possible, on the more unfamiliar nature of Canadian outward investment. Naturally both sides of the story are important.

The major problem for the public policy of substituting foreign direct investment for exporting is that there is a common perception that jobs are lost to Canadians. For example, if National Sea Products faces a countervailing duty on frozen fish in the future, then to protect its U.S. market, it may need to close down some of its processing plants in the Maritimes and open new plants in New England. Such foreign investment creates jobs for Americans and appears to lose jobs in Canada.

However, if such a substitution of foreign direct investment for exporting is the only way for National Sea to service a protectionist U.S. market then the corporate efficiency of this multinational will actually help to maintain jobs in Canada. This occurs in two ways. First, if the U.S. subsidiary purchases a significant amount of imports from the parent (on average the U.S. subsidiaries of all of Canada's multinationals purchase five times as much as they sell back to their parents, see chapter 3). Second, when National Sea earns profits on its foreign operations and when the dividends are paid to Canadian shareholders, thereby creating wealth (and jobs) for Canada. Indeed the process of multinational activity by Canada's large multinationals generates net benefits for Canadians, including an expansion of employment that would otherwise have been lost in a world of intense global competition (Rugman and McIlveen 1985).

The argument that trade and investment are complements (rather than substitutes) obviously does not raise
this issue of a social loss of jobs. Briefly, those taking this
view suggest that liberalization of trade promotes a growth
of economic activity that leads to greater investment opportunities (both domestic and foreign) and greater production
(both domestic and foreign). The EEC experienced rapid increases in both internal trade and direct investment after
its formation and greater inflows of third party investment,
especially from the United States. The implications of the
EEC experience for a U.S.-Canadian bilateral trade agreement are that there will be an increase in intra-firm trade
and production after the agreement, plus greater inflows of
direct investment, probably from Japan and Europe. These
points will be examined in the new empirical work on the
extent of intra-industry trade and production in North
America, reported in chapters 3 and 4.

The literature suggests that the question of whether
trade and direct investment are substitutes or complements
is actually a non-issue. Trade and (portfolio) investment
can be considered as substitutes when considered within
the context of the Heckscher-Ohlin-Samuelson framework,
as by Mundell (1957) and Kemp (1964). However, once the
key characteristics of direct investment are included, such
as intermediate knowledge assets, differentiated products
and scale economies by multi-plant operations, then it becomes obvious that managerial decisions are the critical
considerations.

As is now well known, a large literature on the multinational enterprise postulates that the decision to make a foreign direct investment is an act of strategic management.
To sell products abroad every multinational enterprise can
choose between exporting, direct investment, and non-
equity forms of foreign involvement such as licensing. The
choice is determined by evaluations of the relative costs
and benefits of each modality, see Rugman (1981), Caves
(1982), and Rugman, Lecraw, and Booth (1985) for synthe-
ses and expositions of these basic principles of international business.

In the context of the modern theory of the multinational
enterprise it is apparent that trade and investment are nei-

ther entirely substitutes nor complements. A firm can use either or both methods depending upon the circumstances. There are no absolutes, only a relative cost-benefit analysis to be made, given available information, including the nature of tariff and non-tariff barriers to trade.

Within this framework it is easy to predict the outcome of trade liberalization. Multinationals, from both the United States and Canada, are concerned primarily with secure markets and stable sales. In the present status quo of increased recourse to contingent protection by U.S. rivals, Canadian multinationals will tend to increase their direct investment in the United States as they find exporting becomes more difficult. With trade liberalization (provided it includes the end to such non-tariff barriers to trade) the process will slow down, i.e., there will be a slower rate of increase in Canadian direct investment in the United States. However, existing Canadian investments are highly unlikely to be repatriated due to the existence of exit barriers and the observed successful performance of Canadian subsidiaries to date. For similar reasons U.S. subsidiaries in Canada will not close up after trade liberalization; however there may be a gradual slow down in the rate of increased direct investment.

Safarian (1985) examines the issue of whether or not investment is a substitute or a complement to trade. He considers the effects of a new trading agreement between Canada and the United States on the activities of multinational enterprises. He separates new investment from the activities of existing subsidiaries in each country and then analyzes the individual changes that will occur with respect to: U.S. multinationals with subsidiaries in Canada; Canadian multinationals with subsidiaries in the United States; and third-country multinationals with subsidiaries in either Canada or the United States. He indicates that tariff and non-tariff barriers initially forced companies to locate in Canada. This is an argument that supports investment as being a substitute for trade. However, there are other more relevant features today that override the tariff barrier argument. Safarian uses the modern theory of foreign direct investment to deduce that multinationals invest in other countries in order to profitably utilize knowledge assets within the organizational form of the subsidiary. Internal production is preferred to exporting (or licensing) when there exist constraints such as: the difficulty in transferring technology to a third-party, risk of imitation; the cost of bargaining; after-sales and marketing skills; and the existence of government subsidies and performance requirements.

Since the tariff barrier reason for the location of subsidiaries in Canada may not be as important today, Safarian indicates that removal of these other constraints should allow Canadian manufacturing to rationalize by scaling-up and specializing in fewer product lines. However, due to the increases in competition brought on by the "environment," both Canadian and U.S. multinationals will still invest in the other country in order to capture and maintain their markets. In fact, trade and investment between Canada and the United States will both increase, i.e., complementing each other rather than substituting for one another. The key reasons for this are: (1) that firms tend to trade with their own affiliates due to specialization of subsidiaries and the growth in vertical integration of firms (intra-firm trade); and (2) that in order to deter the threat of increased imports or direct investment, firms will either (i) enter the competitor's market, (ii) export to the competitor's market, (iii) buy out the foreign competitor, or (iv) even become involved in some sort of "collusive" market sharing agreement.

As evidence of the complementarity of trade and investment, Safarian points out the situation that occurred in the EEC, where foreign direct investment expanded rapidly even though barriers were removed. Safarian, however, cautions that unaccounted for non-tariff barriers may have given rise to the same results. Safarian indicates that four factors will help to limit the flow of investment out of Canada. These include: (1) rationalization by U.S. firms that are already here (the sunk cost argument); (2) that secondary Canadian manufacturers will gear up to take advantage of the change; (3) that there will be an expansion in primary resource processing (Canada's comparative advantage); and (4) that there will be increased third-country investment in Canada. If, however, his prognosis is wrong, Safarian presents the argument that the "exodus" will lower the real value of the

Canadian factors of production, which will encourage firms, both Canadian and non-Canadian, to try and produce in Canada since there will be increased opportunities for earning profits.

Building on earlier papers, Burgess (1986) also examines the issue of substitutes and complements. He focuses on three questions concerning the Canada-United States "free" trade talks and the location of Canadian and American firms. These include: (1) would a free trade agreement (FTA) encourage or discourage firms to locate new plants in Canada; (2) would a FTA cause widespread disinvestment by U.S. multinationals currently operating branch plants in Canada behind trade barriers; and (3) would a FTA put many Canadian-owned firms at risk to takeover by large U.S. multinationals who can afford assured access to the U.S. market as well as marketing and distribution expertise.

Burgess makes an analysis of the criteria that should be included in a FTA. In terms of foreign investment he indicates, that except for some basic limitations, a FTA should receive national treatment by the other country. Burgess also reviews the Harris and Cox (1983) computational general equilibrium model. He indicates that the model does not go into the dynamic changes that would occur in the long run, governing the prospect of investment and plant location.

Burgess does not support the notion that exporting and establishing branch plants are substitutes. He argues that the establishment of foreign branch plants as a way of capturing the economic rent from "certain firm-specific intangible costs" is too simplistic an explanation. Rather, subsidiaries are necessary in order to service local individual markets. Also, subsidiary companies tend to trade with each other, buying and selling (vertical and horizontal specialization), components at various stages of processing. In this case, trade and foreign direct investment are complementing each other and not just substituting for one another. In general, Burgess contends that foreign direct investment will be stimulated in both directions with a FTA between Canada and the United States, and that there are no indications it will be biased in one direction or the other.

INTRA-FIRM TRADE

It has been shown that both Safarian (1985) and Burgess (1985, 1986) have reasoned that after the introduction of bilateral free trade there will be an increase in direct investment in the form of intra-firm trade. The conventional view as expressed in the Macdonald Royal Commission report (Canada, 1985) is that the expanded economic opportunities within a North American free trade area will generate economies of scale, leading to greater specialization, more efficient production runs (especially for Canadian producers), and greater bilateral trade. For evidence on the small scale of Canadian plants in the 1970s and some support for the proposition that trade liberalization will increase plant size see Baldwin and Gorecki (1985). For some recent counter evidence, to the effect that Canadian exporters may not increase their degree of specialization, see Balcome (1986).

The nature of business today, however, is different from the neoclassical world of simple comparative advantage and scale economy effects, which would predict greater exports after free trade. Instead, nearly half of the world's international exchange takes place between multinational enterprises (Stopford 1982). The proportion of bilateral intra-firm trade is even higher, at around 70 percent, e.g., see Mac-Charles (1985b, 1987) and the data in chapter 3 of this study. Due to the constraints of today's global competition, economies of scope and strategic positioning are very important to such multinationals. It is apparent that after free trade, both U.S. and Canadian multinationals will need to adopt new business strategies to retain or establish appropriate market shares and to continue to control activities within their internal markets. It is in this sense that North American intra-firm trade would be expected to expand in the form of both an increase in final and intermediate products.

Evidence that such expansion occurred in the EEC can be found in Franko (1977), Aquino (1978), Giersch (1979), and Balassa (1986). The implications of the EEC experience for Canada have been discussed by Lane (1986) and Mac-Charles (1985a, 1985b). Here this work is used as a basis for new research on the extent of bilateral intra-industry trade in chapters 3 and 4 while the previous work is extended by analysis of specific multinationals and the way in which their strategic planning function operates, in Chapters 5–7.

MacCharles (1985a) examined the extent of domestic and international intra-industry trade (IIT) for Canada. Mac-Charles finds that the small market size in Canada has encouraged horizontal and vertical diversification on a greater scale than in other countries. The high degree of horizontal and vertical diversification has in fact, added to unit costs of Canadian manufacturing due to diseconomies of scale. His evidence appears to indicate that Canadian-owned firms have been adjusting faster than U.S. subsidiaries to new trade strategies. Canadian firms have been increasing the degree of specialization and their propensity to export over the 1970s faster than the U.S. subsidiaries in Canada. In fact, he finds that U.S. firms, until recently were continuing to diversify rather than specializing in fewer product lines.

Another factor to be considered is that of non-North American investment, especially as it may respond to a bilateral trade agreement. Due to the vitality of such an expanded North American economy greater inflows of European, Japanese, and other overseas direct investment can be expected. Such investment should be motivated by the expanded market opportunities in North America. In this situation Canada might expect to receive more than a proportionate share of such investment, since there will be access to the U.S. market via Canada.

However, with bilateral trade liberalization it is anticipated that Canada will retain its sovereignty, tax system, exchange rate, culture, and other attributes of the nation. This distinctiveness of Canadian political, cultural, and social institutions (from the viewpoint of a foreign investor), reduces the political risk of investing in the United States while not compromising the economic return. Thus Canadian sovereignty becomes an economic asset in a world where the principles of international diversification still matter. The extent to which such political and social diversification affects "third party" investment in North America is not the primary focus of this study and is largely ignored here. Therefore the beneficial effects of such investment inflows will mean that the adjustment costs of bilateral trade liberalization are overestimated in this study.

U.S. SUBSIDIARIES IN CANADA

Concern has been expressed that U.S.-owned multinationals will close up their Canadian subsidiaries after free trade. The argument is that many U.S. multinationals originally came to Canada to jump its tariff wall, but the postwar liberalization of trade in the seven GATT rounds has reduced this incentive. Yet there are still a larger number of U.S. subsidiaries in Canada. Why is this? Partly it is due to the sunk costs of having established factories and businesses that involved discrete investment decisions that are difficult to liquidate once conditions change. This is a type of exit barrier discussed in the literature on strategic planning by analysts such as Porter (1980). But of greater importance is the changing nature of foreign direct investment today.

It has been demonstrated in Dunning and Rugman (1985) that a major motivation for foreign direct investment is the need to overcome transaction costs and other exogenous natural market imperfections, an explanation that is entirely separate from the tariff argument. To an increasing degree, modern multinationals compete on economies of scope whereby they need to customize products for segments of national markets and utilize modular assembly and flexible manufacturing systems to combine production efficiency with marketing intelligence. Such in-house production and marketing skills are fostered by management teams operating within carefully designed organizational structures that bridge national jurisdictions. This process of internalization, in response to exogenous transaction costs, is an efficient company response and this motivation for multinational operations will continue even after a bilateral free trade area is introduced.

It is necessary to work this modern theory of the multinational enterprise into studies of the adjustment problems stemming from trade liberalization. Most of the general equilibrium models fail to incorporate aspects of intermediate knowledge advantages into their structure and they are thereby poor predictors of the effects of freer trade. Harris (1985) has calculated that the short-term effect of bilateral free trade will be a 5.5 percent increase in employment, with even larger gains in the long run after adjustment is completed. The Harris finding takes into account the fact that capital is internationally mobile whereas labour is less mobile; thus under free trade the return to capital is fixed and any gains from increased output go to labour. He also attempts to incorporate aspects of multinationality, such as scale economies, but his, and related models, need to be rethought to find out if more critical components of internalization can be incorporated.

This point becomes even clearer when it is remembered that we are moving towards a service economy. In Canada today 70 percent of employment is in service industries. Most services are consumed internally, so the amount of services involved in bilateral trade is much lower, at 20 percent (Stern 1985). The nature of a service is that it must be delivered by the producer to the customer. In the context of trade today, this frequently requires the involvement of a multinational enterprise, since only within such a firm can quality control be maintained.

After bilateral free trade we would expect to observe a large increase in traded service activities, especially in the financial and human capital services characteristic of multinational enterprises. This expansion of traded service activity will generate many relatively highly paid jobs for Canadians, provided that there is good management education and related training programmes. Again, the nature of intangible service activities can be incorporated into trade models by recognizing the powerful predictions of internalization theory, which deals with such intangible intermediate products.

Baranson (1985) examines the impact of free trade on U.S. branch plants in Canada, which came here, he states, to avoid the Canadian tariff. On the basis of a simplistic production function focus on high technology and computer integrated manaufacturing he argues that U.S. branch plants in Canada will be replaced by more efficient plants in the U.S. South. He predicts that the development of technologically efficient "clusters" in the U.S. South will pull the branch plants out of Canada, which has higher labour costs and lower productivity. He states that the branch plants in

Canada lack management and marketing skills to partici-
pate in the economies-of-scope—driven systems that U.S.
firms will need to adopt to remain internationally competitive. In particular, flexible manufacturing systems and more
versatile production will not come from the U.S. branch
plants.

It is apparent from this study that Baranson knows little
about Canada and that a simple examination of the facts
would invalidate his predictions. For example, he ignores
Canadian multinationals and states that U.S. branch plants
account for two-thirds of the Canadian manufacturing industry with sales over $250 million. Yet, examination of the
Financial Post 500 ("Industry's 500" 1986) reveals that
only about 30 percent of Canada's largest firms are actually
U.S.-owned. The only Canadian-owned multinational mentioned by Baranson is Northern Telecom, whereas there are
many other Canadian multinationals that are already using
successful technologies.

The conceptual problems with Baranson's work are his
one-dimensional focus upon the production function, which
ignores the modern-day importance of marketing, especially its strategic importance, discussed in recent works
on Canadian multinationals, such as that of Rugman and
McIlveen (1985) and by Litvak and Maule (1981). There already exist many successful Canadian-owned multinationals (in addition to Northern Telecom). Both Abitibi-Price
and Domtar, Inc. have integrated, computer-controlled paper
mills. Moore Corporation Limited has taken flexible manufacturing to a high level with on-site printing of small business forms in its Moore Business Centre stores. It is expanding its telemarketing efforts and it has computer-
controlled production in its main production facilities
(Rugman and McIlveen 1985).

Baranson's argument, that the majority of U.S. branch
plants will leave Canada, is wrong from the point of view of
both the niching and marketing arguments for location. It
also fails to take into account non-tariff barriers. Only government procurement is identified in his analysis as such a
barrier. But nominal tariff barriers today would do little to
explain why there are so many foreign subsidiaries in Canada. Therefore, in order to explain rationalization under free

trade, an explanation of what will happen to non-tariff barriers to trade also has to be put forward.

Baranson argues that U.S. industry will cluster to the U.S. South leaving only Canadian firms still serving the Canada market in "specialty" areas, with all major production originating from the U.S. South. Yet Canadian firms or even U.S. branch plants could cluster in Southern Ontario (Wonnacott 1986). Most Canadian centres are in fact no farther away from the huge U.S. eastern seaboard market than the South is to the major U.S. market. Canadian companies are in fact just as likely to produce for the larger market as are American firms in the same position.

Chisholm (1985) reviewed the incidence of tariff protection among 20 manufacturing sectors in Canada with the incidence of the level of foreign ownership. His proposition was, that if tariff protection is an important cause of foreign direct investment, the pattern of sectoral incidence of tariffs should mirror the sectoral incidence of foreign control across all 20 sectors. After considering the pattern for 1970, 1975, and 1978, Chisholm concluded that the pattern is incompatible with a close causal relationship between tariff protection and foreign ownership within the Canadian manufacturing sector. In general, reduced tariff barriers would not have a major impact on the overall level of foreign direct investment in Canada.

It has been argued by economists such as Safarian (1985) and Wolf (1984) that with a bilateral free trade agreement there will be incentives for U.S. subsidiaries in Canada to expand production using world product mandates. I am on record elsewhere as being extremely wary of the possibility of U.S. multinationals wishing to dole out such world product mandates to the Canadian subsidiaries (Rugman 1983a). This analysis demonstrated the increased risks to the parent multinational's firm-specific advantages of such a policy of decentralized research and development (R & D), production, and marketing. However, it was based on an interpretation of public policy whereby Canadian federal and provincial R & D subsidies would be restricted to subsidiaries with a world product mandate. The analysis did not consider the adaptability of the subsidiaries to changes in the

North American trading environment, especially where discriminatory subsidies were not the issue.

Perhaps a more fruitful way of looking at this is to recognize that under a free trade agreement there will be greater opportunities for investment by Canadian-owned firms over foreign-owned firms in Canada. Today the latter consist of many subsidiaries that are more than branch plants attracted by the tariff. Many U.S.-owned subsidiaries in Canada employ good managers, trained human capital, and enthusiastic workers who may be well equipped to adapt to new market opportunities in North America.

On the issue of investment and U.S. subsidiary production in Canada, Simon Reisman (1985, 393) has noted that under free trade what would occur would be "changes in product mix, more specialization, longer runs and increases in scale. World-mandating for selected products would become a more common practice, and we would likely see mergers and takeovers as the more energetic and enterprising firms responded to market opportunities." For this to occur and generate more jobs with trade liberalization will require a response by the key multinationals; the managerial implications of such adjustment are explored in chapters 5 to 7 of this study.

CANADIAN OUTWARD DIRECT INVESTMENT

Much of Canada's foreign direct investment is undertaken by a group of mature and resource-based multinationals such as Alcan, Seagram, Noranda, Consolidated-Bathurst, Bombardier, and others, listed in chapter 5 of this study. Only 1 of the largest 21 Canadian multinationals has the traditional R & D based firm-specific advantage of multinationals. This is Northern Telecom. The others have firm-specific advantages based on a value-added chain of resource-based harvesting, processing, and marketing. Indeed the marketing skills are perhaps the most important asset as these firms seek niches for new product lines.

The implication of this analysis is that Canadian outward investment will continue after a bilateral free trade area is implemented. The reasons for multinational activity have more to do with internal managerial decisions about restructuring and rationalization of the firm than with outside policy-induced factors. To a degree, some of these large Canadian-owned multinationals have been concerned about access to the U.S. market in the face of contingent protectionism. Most of the larger Canadian multinationals have already resolved this problem by entry to the United States in the form of subsidiary production, joint ventures, or acquisitions.

Based on analysis of the motives for Canadian outward investment reported in Rugman (1987) it can be predicted that now that the Canadian multinationals are in the U.S. market they will not leave. This partly reflects the asymmetry of size between Canada and the United States. For a Canadian firm to produce in the United States is a bigger corporate commitment than for a U.S. firm to enter Canada. There are exit barriers as well as entry barriers in being in a market ten times larger than Canada's. Under free trade Canadian-owned multinationals will retain their U.S. subsidiaries due to exit barriers and sunk costs. However, future investment decisions in a broader North American free market will be made in a new environment where exporting from Canada may become attractive once again.

The recent growth of Canadian direct investment in the United States is also due to another factor. This is the growing degree of cross-investments on a worldwide basis, identified in chapter 1. Within this global phenomenon of growing cross-investments, greater North American and world economic integration, and the rise of multinational enterprises, it can be predicted that the nature of a comprehensive bilateral trade agreement will be to faciliate further beneficial economic interdependence, in which efficiency and wealth are increased. The impact of a trade agreement, presumably, will be to stabilize the rules of the game, nurturing efficient long-run investment decisions by the managers of North American multinationals. This should have beneficial impacts on jobs, savings, wealth generation, and political stability. This analysis relies on the arguments that trade and investments are complementary and that within a free trade area, governments can provide stable parameters for the strategic planners of multinational enterprises to make efficient internal decisions.

STRATEGIC PLANNING AND THE ADJUSTMENT PROCESS

The idea that the presence of multinational enterprises could mitigate the costs of implementing a free-trade area is one that has not yet been incorporated into formal economic models of adjustment. The general equilibrium trade models of structural adjustment used by economists have been modified, especially by Harris (1985), to take into account some of the key characteristics of multinationality, e.g., scale economies and product differentiation. However, these models have not attempted to evaluate internal managerial decisions about restructuring and rationalization, i.e., they have not addressed the central issue of strategy and structure within the multinational enterprise.

We know that all multinationals today have elaborate systems for strategic planning. At the simplest level such strategic planning requires an analysis of exogenous environmental parameters, for example by country risk assessments and political risk analysis, coupled with endogenous internal factors related to the company's costs and productivity across its functional areas.

If the bulk of U.S.-Canadian trade is indeed intra-firm and conducted by 200 to 300 large U.S.-owned and Canadian-owned multinationals then the strategic planning "departments" of these firms will be the places to look for corporate reactions to the impact of a bilateral trade agreement. It is in the self-interest of the firms to minimize disruption caused by a new trade regime, so the decisions made by strategic planners to reposition product lines, restructure operations and alter subsidiary outputs, will be efficient signals for public policy makers to observe.

It follows that an important conclusion of this study is that the elasticity of trade, investment, and production with respect to trade liberalization is a dynamic concept, which can only be captured by an examination of the strategic management of the firm. In order to anticipate these reactions a supplementary study is undertaken in chapter 7. The strategic planners of major multinationals were asked to predict company responses to a comprehensive bilateral free trade agreement. This analysis was based on a structured questionnaire sent to CEOs and other top managers responsible for strategic planning.

EVIDENCE ON THE DETERMINANTS OF FOREIGN DIRECT INVESTMENT

A number of previous surveys have been carried out to identify the main determinants of investment in Canada by U.S. firms and of investment in the United States by Canadian firms. Four surveys are reviewed by the Department of External Affairs (1985a):

1. a Conference Board of Canada study by McDonald (1984)
2. a Department of External Affairs study (1985b)
3. the C. D. Howe Institute study by Forget and Denis (1985)
4. the International Business Council of Canada study by Matheson (1985)

The results of these surveys are important since there is a different impact on U.S. subsidiaries in Canada compared to Canadian affiliates in the United States. Investment decisions for the former, often referred to as branch plants, are found to be not much affected by tariff or non-tariff barriers to trade. Instead, broader variables reflecting market growth and profitability are the key determinants. On the other hand, Canadian direct investment in the United States is influenced much more strongly by problems of market access.

These results, discussed below in more detail, have two major implications. First, it is apparent that trade liberalization will *not* lead to major closures of U.S.-owned plants in Canada. The survey evidence suggests that removal of trade barriers will have a broadly neutral impact on such U.S. direct investment in Canada. Therefore there will not be major job losses and adjustment costs in the foreign-owned sector. Second, Canadian outward direct investment is more sensitive to U.S. trade barriers, so trade liberalization may slow down the role of investment outflows and stimulate more exports. This will generate more employment in Canada, although the impact will probably be fairly small since the direct investment outflows were efficiency-based and did not actually cause job losses in Canada.

The overall impact of both effects is also small and the general conclusion is that direct investment flows are not greatly affected by trade liberalization. If this is the case, then adjustment problems and employment effects are also small. This reflects the extent to which multinational enterprises have already helped to bypass barriers to trade and integrate the two economies. Naturally when trade liberalization does occur there will be fewer disruptive elements, due to the stabilizing role played by multinationals.

The Conference Board of Canada (McDonald 1984) survey was based on a questionnaire sent to 7,500 potential foreign investors in Canada from 19 foreign countries. The survey contained 21 criteria that might have affected the most recent decision to invest or not to invest in Canada. One problem with this type of survey is that by giving a range of possible answers, it constrains the respondent to identify one of the listed responses, while the foreign investor may not have actually considered them until the questionnaire appeared. This presents a challenge to those who design such research instruments.

The Conference Board survey identified three groups of factors: market factors, competitive factors, and environmental factors. They found that market factors such as market growth and industry profitability provided the greatest incentive to invest in Canada. An interesting result was that tariff/non-tariff barriers were rated as having a neutral impact on the inward investment decision. Perhaps non-tariff barriers should have been broken down into their component parts, since in the survey they were being captured by some of the other components, such as: foreign investment controls, government regulations, government incentives, and taxation factors.

A survey of 200 large corporations that have Canadian subsidiaries, was also carried out by the Department of External Affairs (1985b). The survey attempted to assess three business attitudes towards investment decisions: First, the factors determining investment over the next five to ten years; second, the importance of tariff and non-tariff barriers as a factor in determining investment in Canada and the United States during the next five to ten years; and third the impact of tariff elimination on future investment plans. The determinants of the investment decision were split into factors that were either market related, competitiveness related, or environmentally related (the latter including being either political/regulatory related or economically related). The study found that political/regulatory factors, cost considerations, and trade barriers, in that order, were the most frequently mentioned factors governing the investment decision.

Further analysis of trade barriers revealed that, while trade barriers were considered important by over one-half of the firms surveyed, only one-quarter felt that the elimination of trade barriers would alter their investment decision. In general, the results appear to support the Conference Board of Canada findings that trade barriers are not a significant factor in determining investment in Canada.

However, one of the major inconsistencies in both studies is that they find that foreign firms consider government regulation, market access, tax regimes, and government incentives to be significant determinants of foreign investment. Yet, three of these factors are actually non-tariff barriers to trade. This problem occurs in all surveys that do not distinguish properly between traditional tariff barriers, and what are today an increasing galaxy of non-tariff barriers. In fact, what many analysts and managers may perceive as environmental or other barriers can in many cases be considered as non-tariff barriers. This is a problem of classification in questionnaires designed to determine the factors governing the foreign direct investment decision.

The Forget and Denis (1985) survey for the C. D. Howe Institute, of the total population of outward direct investors, was designed to find the attitudes of Canadian firms towards direct investment in the United States. Primary industries tended to rate access to raw materials, market size, and corporate taxation as major reasons for investing in the United States. Non-primary industries rated market potential, market size, and proximity to customers as important investment reasons. In general, U.S. pull factors explained 85 percent of the motives for Canadian direct investment in the United States whereas Canadian push factors explained only 15 percent of outward investment.

The results of the survey on tariff and non-tariff barriers indicated that one-third of the firms felt them to be very important or important in influencing their investment decisions. Manufacturing industries rated the importance of

tariff and non-tariff barriers as much more important than
did the other types of industries. It was indicated that both
types of trade barriers would double in importance as a
factor that would influence investment decisions in five
years time. This may be an indication that Canadian firms
believe that the level of trade barriers between Canada
and the United States is increasing and not decreasing in
importance.

In terms of production, 70 percent of the firms produced
the same goods or services as their parent firms in Canada.
Eighty-one percent of them had not engaged in licensing
and had located in the United States to overcome trade barriers and to be close to their markets. Higher Canadian production costs did not appear to be a major factor. Of the 70
percent, more than half had never exported. Over 50 percent
of those firms that had previously exported believed that
their exports would have been smaller to the United States
if they had not developed a U.S. operation.

One of the major findings of the Forget and Davis survey
was that Canadian subsidiaries in the United States have
a higher propensity to import goods from Canada than
U.S. firms (a point confirmed in chapters 3 and 4) and that
more than half of their Canadian imports consist of final goods. This would indicate that foreign direct investment in the United States by Canadian firms does not cost
Canada as many jobs as the level of outward investment
would first indicate. (These issues are discussed in detail in
chapter 5.)

Matheson (1985) conducted a survey of 18 Canadian
multinationals to find their reasons for investing in the
United States between 1980 and 1984. Ten of the firms surveyed had sales of greater than $1 million. There were five
major reasons given by the Canadian firms for investing
in the United States. These were split into those governing
fast growing industries and those governing slower growth
industries. For the fast-growth industries, overcoming trade
barriers and serving the market were the main reasons
for investing, while for the slow-growth industries, modifying the production process, strengthening the existing business, and diversifying into other businesses were listed as
the most important reasons for investing in the United
States.

The survey also indicated that Canadian companies that invested in the United States still invested in Canada. Most of the foreign investment was in fact unique and would not have taken place in Canada anyway, since it was carried out to gain further export opportunities, which would not have occurred if the firms had invested that capital in Canada. In fact, the study indicated that most of the Canadian foreign investment was in the acquisition of American firms, rather than in the building of new concerns.

From the latter two studies it would appear that, while tariff barriers have diminished in importance, there is still a concern by Canadian firms that in order to respond or to maintain their market opportunities it is necessary to have direct investment in the United States. This is an indication that non-tariff barriers have been of importance in accelerating Canadian foreign direct investment. Non-tariff barriers in the United States such as federal, state and local procurement policies; regulatory standards; and anti-dumping and countervail procedures, are avoided by producing or selling through a U.S. subsidiary rather than exporting directly from Canada.

A survey of investment determinants for smaller Canadian multinationals was carried out by Litvak and Maule (1981). Their results indicate that the major reason why the 25 companies invested was the pull factor of gaining access to the U.S. market. This was similar to the key reason for investing given by larger Canadian multinational firms.

At least three other studies of the determinants of direct investment in the United States have also been carried out: the Group of Thirty study (1984); the U.S. Department of Commerce study (1985b); and Gandhi's (1984) regional study. These are reviewed in chapter 3 of Rugman (1987).

The 1985 U.S. Department of Commerce study, *Foreign Direct Investment in the United States: Completed Transactions, 1974–1983*, attributed foreign direct investment to the generally favourable climate found in the United States during the late 1970s and the 1980–1981 period. This study identified five major attributes that contributed to the investment climate, including:

1. relative U.S. political and economic stability
2. the sheer size and strength of the U.S. economy

3. the emergence of large companies based abroad with
the resources needed to become active multinational corporations
4. a relatively non-restrictive U.S. policy toward foreign direct investment
5. the low value of the dollar during the 1978–80 period

The Commerce study found that the majority of direct
investment in the United States was accounted for by the
major industrialized countries, with Canada being the largest single source of foreign direct investment transactions
during the 1976–1983 period. Three-fifths of the foreign direct investment transactions during the period were in the
manufacturing and real property sectors. Canada, along
with investors from the Netherlands accounted for most of
the growth in real property investment (non-agricultural
land, hotels, office buildings, etc.), between 1976 and 1981.

After 1981 the study indicated that direct investment in
the United States slowed down. The Commerce Department
attributes the 37 percent decline in inward direct investment from 1981 to 1983 to a lagged response to the recession by the United States and other industrialized countries
during the 1981–1982 period. Also, the appreciation of the
U.S. dollar during the same period reduced investment because of the increased cost to foreigners of acquiring U.S.
assets.

A 1984 study, *Foreign Direct Investment 1973–87*, by
The Group of Thirty, assessed the determinants of direct investment by 50 large U.S. and European multinationals.
Four major reasons for investment, in decreasing order of
importance, were given by the corporations:

1. To gain access to domestic or regional markets
2. To integrate foreign operations with existing investments; or to adapt to structural changes in the industry
3. To avoid trade barriers
4. To seek out faster-growing markets abroad

These results are similar to Matheson's (1985) results
for the International Business Council of Canada. Both
studies found that it is important to gain access to the market, and also to strengthen, restructure, or diversify the
business in order to remain internationally competitive.

A study of Canadian direct investment in the state of New York was carried out by Gandhi (1984). He found that 81 percent of firms invested in New York State due to its nearness to the parent firm; 79 percent indicated that the location provided them with good potential for growth in the United States; 77 percent invested there because of the area; while 64 percent invested there because of its good transportation infrastructure, in particular, highways.

Most of the firms in the Gandhi study were small; only 15 percent had assets in excess of $9 million. The small size of the Canadian firms may have hindered them in their ability to export efficiently to the United States. Rather than wasting corporate resources in exporting attempts, it was easier to develop manufacturing capability directly in the United States. The general indications are that the overall size and attractiveness of the U.S. market appears to have been the major reason for locating in New York State, along with the potential positive attitude put forward by the state to attract new investment during the recession years of the early 1980s.

Chapter 3

The Patterns of Bilateral Foreign Direct Investment

This chapter examines the extent of bilateral direct investment. The first half of the chapter considers the performance of U.S. subsidiaries in Canada. A major finding in this section is that, on average, the U.S. subsidiaries export about one-quarter of their output—a fact often neglected by persons who view foreign-owned subsidiaries in Canada as being in import-competing sectors. The second half of the chapter reports new data on the performance of Canadian-owned affiliates in the United States. It is found that these Canadian multinationals purchase, on average, five times as much from their parent firms in Canada as they "export" back to Canada.

The presentation of material in this chapter emphasizes the conceptual linkages between examination of the performance of U.S. subsidiaries in Canada and Canadian affiliates in the United States. There has been an unfortunate tendency to concentrate on the former and neglect the latter. Only when both elements of direct investment are considered can the impact of bilateral trade liberalization be predicted. The material considered here will be used as a basis for further work in chapter 4, where the balance of bilateral intra-firm trade will be analyzed.

BILATERAL TRADE PERFORMANCE OF U.S.-OWNED SUBSIDIARIES IN CANADA

There is still a common perception by many Canadians that foreign-owned firms, which were often set up originally to bypass the Canadian tariff, are still branch plants selling entirely within the Canadian market. This perception is inaccurate. The foreign-owned subsidiaries are in practice involved in as much international trade activity as domestically-owned corporations. For example, in 1981, the largest 300 foreign-owned companies in Canada exported nearly one-quarter of their output.

52

The data source for this section is the annual survey on *Foreign-Owned Subsidiaries in Canada*. This survey was started over 20 years ago to help the Government of Canada monitor the economic performance of foreign-owned companies, in accordance with the so-called "Winter" guidelines of 31 March 1966. Winter was the Minister of Industry, Trade and Commerce (IT&C) at that time, and his department became responsible for the collection of data based on an annual questionnaire. IT&C's work was reinforced by the "Gillespie" guidelines of 1975, which followed the passage of Phase II of the Foreign Investment Review Act.

The questionnaire is sent to the entire set of the largest non-financial foreign-owned subsidiaries in Canada, defined as those with sales of $5 million or greater and foreign ownership of 50 percent or more. There are usually about 300 such respondents, which covers the activities of about 1,000 separate companies (since some firms consolidate returns for a number of affiliate companies). In the last year for which data were collected, a total of 274 companies responded on behalf of a "stable total of between 970 to 1,000 respondents." The last report, produced by the Department of Regional Industrial Expansion (DRIE) which contains part of the now defunct IT&C, was published in September 1984 and contains information up to 1981.

Data for subsequent years were collected by Statistics Canada but are still in raw form and have not been published nor made available to independent researchers. Beginning with the 1983 and 1984 questionnaires the data was integrated into CALURA data. Unfortunately, because of the new regulatory changes in 1985 governing the collection of data from corporations, the collection and presentation of these data at the firm level has been virtually eliminated. Further, these data are increasingly integrated with tax data, which are now used by Statistics Canada to supply the same information. Tax data, of course, are confidential and not available to independent researchers.

THE BALANCE OF TRADE FOR U.S. SUBSIDIARIES IN CANADA

Table 3.1 reports data on the balance of trade on foreign sales (X) and purchases (M) for all reporting U.S. subsidiary

Table 3.1

Intra-Industry Trade by U.S. Subsidiaries in Canada: 1964–1981
(millions C$)

Year	Foreign Sales by U.S. Subsidiaries in Canada	Foreign Purchases by U.S. Subsidiaries in Canada (a) (b)	Canadian Balance
1981	20,305	22,389	(2,084)
1980	19,417	20,193	(776)
1979	18,844	20,624	(1,780)
1978	18,013	18,076	(63)
1977	15,261	15,614	(353)
1976	13,173	13,815	(642)
1975	11,459	11,736	(277)
1974	9,846	10,628	(782)
1973	8,177	8,017	160
1972	7,193	6,456	737
1971	6,575	5,760	815
1970	5,688	4,864	824
1969	5,568	5,066	502
1968	4,920	4,422	498
1967	4,025	3,591	434
1966	3,388	2,968	420
1965	2,486	2,445	41
1964	2,278	1,898	380

Notes: (a) The merchandise imports and exports are those made directly by the respondents, and hence, goods sold by them in Canada and subsequently exported are not included in their export figures and imported goods purchased from Canadian suppliers are excluded from their imports.

(b) Import figures include duties, sales taxes and the cost of transportation in Canada, in most cases.

Sources: Canada, Department of Regional Industrial Expansion, Foreign-Owned Subsidiaries in Canada: 1979–1981 (Ottawa: Surveys and Analysis, Statistical and Data Base Services, DRIE, September, 1984): Table 13.

Canada, Department of Industry, Trade and Commerce, Foreign-Owned Subsidiaries in Canada, [various years] (Ottawa: Statistical and Data Base Services, IT & C (DRIE), April 1983, May 1975, 1974, August 1972, and 1970): Table 13, Appendix VII and Summary Table 27.

corporations in Canada covered by the IT&C and DRIE survey.

The term intra-industry trade is used to define trade between foreign-owned affiliates and all their trading partners. The term is distinguished from intra-firm trade (used later in tables 3.2, 3.4, and 3.5), which is defined as internal trade between the subsidiary and its parent. The measure of intra-industry trade is of course a proxy for intra-industry trade. The analysis is not broken down for sales by one firm in a given industry to another in the same industry. This proxy is, however, justified on at least two grounds. Mac-Charles (1987) has used the Grubel-Lloyd index (explained in chapter 4 of this book) to measure intra-industry trade. While his work is at the industry level and is not aggregated, the high rates recorded suggest that sales by multinational firms are largely to firms in the same industry. Secondly, the data presented subsequently in chapter 4 also support the above definition of intra-industry trade.

Table 3.1 reports data on intra-industry trade. Between 1964 and 1973 the balance of trade was favourable to Canada, but since 1974, foreign purchases by the U.S. subsidiaries have remained larger than foreign sales. Over the 5 year period, from 1977 to 1981, foreign sales have averaged Cdn. $18.4 billion, while foreign purchases have averaged Cdn. $19.4 billion, for an average deficit of Cdn. $1.0 billion. (The total deficit is Cdn. $5 billion for these five years.)

The decline in growth in foreign sales was particularly responsibile for the larger than normal deficits in 1979 and 1981. Foreign sales growth between 1979 and 1981 averaged 4 percent, while for the earlier period 1974 to 1978, it averaged 17 percent (an average growth of 12 percent over the entire 1974–1981 period). For purchases over the same periods: from 1979 to 1981 they averaged 8 percent, and 18 percent for 1974 to 1978 (an average growth of 14 percent for the entire 1974–1981 period).

Over the 1964–1981 period, the growth of foreign sales and purchases by the U.S. subsidiaries in Canada has remained relatively stable; averaging 14 percent for sales and 16 percent for purchases. The growth in foreign purchases has, however, been more susceptible to decline than exports, though this phenomenon appears to have been confined to the early 1970s. Purchases declined 4 percent in 1970, and there was also a small decline in 1980 of 2 percent.

The most important interpretation to be drawn from table 3.1 is the approximate balance between imports and exports by foreign-owned subsidiaries in Canada. These U.S. affiliates are not purely branch plants, importing components and knowledge from their parents and selling their entire output in the Canadian host market. Instead they export nearly as much as they import. This is a remarkable performance if the classic theoretical reason for foreign direct investment in Canada (the tariff) is correct.

It is argued that high Canadian tariffs, first imposed to protect domestic industry at the time of the National Policy and subsequently maintained, caused a switch to foreign direct investment in Canada, from exporting, as foreign firms (mainly American) sought to jump the tariff wall. The result was (allegedly) branch plants that were miniature replicas of their parents. Obviously these foreign-owned subsidiaries were supposed to be in import-competing sectors. Yet, for the last 20 years, these U.S. subsidiaries have exported as much as they imported—hardly confirmation of the branch plant hypothesis. Rather, these subsidiaries embody characteristics of modern multinationals, in which two-way flows of direct investment (intra-industry trade) are common. This evidence for such intra-industry trade and investment is explored further below.

The relative stability in the growth of foreign sales and purchases by the U.S. subsidiaries in Canada can also be seen in table 3.2. This table shows the ratio of foreign sales and purchases to all (both foreign and Canadian) sales of the U.S. subsidiaries in Canada. Over the ten years, from 1972 to 1981, these percentages have remained remarkably stable, averaging 25.47 percent for foreign to total sales (exports) and 26.19 percent for foreign to total purchases (imports). These ratios are 25.54 percent and 26.85 percent, respectively, for the five years between 1977 and 1981.

The import and export ratios in table 3.2, for the period between 1964 and 1972, confirm the earlier indication that U.S. subsidiaries in Canada, rather than being in branch plant operations (which only service the Canadian mar-

Table 3.2

Ratios of Foreign Sales and Foreign Purchases by
U.S. Subsidiaries in Canada
1965–1981

Year	Foreign Sales as a Percentage of Total Sales	Foreign Purchases as a Percentage of Total Purchases
	%	%
1981	24.84	27.39
1980	24.23	25.19
1979	24.89	27.24
1978	27.39	27.48
1977	26.35	26.96
1976	25.64	26.89
1975	24.80	25.40
1974	24.73	26.70
1973	25.51	25.01
1972	26.28	23.59
1971	26.86	23.53
1970	26.78	22.90
1969	26.27	23.90
1968	25.01	20.86
1967	22.48	20.06
1966	N/A	N/A
1965	N/A	N/A
1964	17.86	14.89

Notes: N/A = Not Available.

Sources: Canada, Department of Regional Industrial Expansion, *Foreign-Owned Subsidiaries in Canada: 1979–1981* (Ottawa: Surveys and Analysis, Statistical and Data Base Services, DRIE, September, 1984): Tables 12 and 13.

Canada, Department of Industry, Trade and Commerce, Foreign-Owned Subsidiaries in Canada, various years (Ottawa: Statistical and Data Base Services, IT & C (DRIE), April 1983, May 1975, 1974, August 1972 and 1970). Tables 1, Summary Table 2 and Summary Table 27.

kets), have consistently sold (exported) approximately 25 percent of their production. Most of these exports go to the United States, in particular back to their parent groups in the United States, as is shown in the data in tables 3.3 and 3.4.

Table 3.3

Intra-Firm Trade by U.S. Subsidiaries in Canada
(millions C$)

Year	Sales by U.S. Subsidiaries in Canada to their Parent Groups (a) (b)	Purchases by U.S. Subsidiaries in Canada from their Parent Groups (a)	Canadian Balance
1981	14,647	15,718	(1,071)
1980	13,347	14,353	(1,006)
1979	13,715	15,639	(1,924)
1978	13,793	13,342	451
1977	11,667	11,357	310
1976	9,953	9,944	9
1975	8,097	8,014	83
1974	7,036	7,253	(217)
1973	6,190	5,891	299
1972	5,389	4,948	441
1971	4,848	4,192	656
1970	4,188	3,352	836
1969	4,216	3,553	663
1968	3,413	3,072	341
1967	2,707	2,310	397
1966	2,006	1,938	68
1965	1,195	1,546	(351)
1964	1,025	1,173	(148)

Notes: (a) The merchandise imports and exports are those made directly by the respondents, and hence, goods sold by them in Canada and subsequently exported are not included in their export figures and imported goods purchased from Canadian suppliers are excluded from their imports.

(b) Import figures include duties, sales taxes and the cost of transportation in Canada, in most cases.

Sources: Canada, Department of Regional Industrial Expansion, *Foreign-Owned Subsidiaries in Canada 1979–1981* (Ottawa: Surveys and Analysis, Statistical and Data Base Services, DRIE, September, 1984): Tables 1, 8 and 14.

Canada, Department of Industry, Trade and Commerce, *Foreign-Owned Subsidiaries in Canada* [various years] (Ottawa: Statistical and Data Base Services, IT&C (DRIE), April 1983, May 1975 and 1974): Tables 1, 3, 8, 14, and Appendix VIII.

Table 3.3 presents data on the intra-firm trade by the affiliates of U.S. multinationals operating in Canada, which consist of sales by U.S. subsidiaries in Canada to their parent groups (x_p) and purchases by the U.S. subsidiaries from their parent groups (M_p). The balance of intra-firm trade is very similar in size to that reported for the intra-industry trade balance in table 3.1. From 1977 to 1981 U.S. parent-

Table 3.4

Intra-Firm Trade Ratios for the
U.S. Subsidiaries in Canada

Year	Sales to the Parent Groups as a Percentage of all Foreign Sales	Purchases from the Parent Groups as a Percentage of all Foreign Purchases
1981	72.13	70.20
1980	68.74	71.08
1979	72.78	75.83
1978	76.57	73.81
1977	76.65	72.74
1976	75.56	71.98
1975	70.66	68.29
1974	71.46	68.24
1973	75.70	73.48
1972	74.92	76.64
1971	73.73	72.78
1970	73.63	68.91
1969	75.72	70.13
1968	69.37	69.47
1967	67.25	64.33
1966	59.21	65.30
1965	48.07	63.23
1964	45.00	61.87

Sources: Canada, Department of Regional Industrial Expansion, *Foreign-Owned Subsidiaries in Canada: 1979–1981* (Ottawa: Surveys and Analysis, Statistical and Data Base Services, DRIE, September, 1984): Tables 1, 8, 13 and 14.

Canada, Department of Industry, Trade and Commerce, Foreign-Owned Subsidiaries in Canada, [various years] (Ottawa: Statistical and Data Base Services, IT & C (DRIE), April 1983, May 1975, 1974, August 1972 and 1970). Tables 1, 8, 3, 13, 14, Summary Table 27, Appendix VII and Appendix VIII.

subsidiary trade resulted in an average deficit for Canada of
Cdn. $828 million, versus the average deficit of Cdn. $1.0
billion for all U.S. subsidiary trade, as was indicated when
discussing table 3.1. In the period from 1977 to 1981, the
growth rates for intra-firm (U.S. parent-subsidiary) trade
were virtually identical at 9.46 and 10.04 percent for sales
and purchases, respectively. However, over the period from
1964 to 1981, exports from the U.S. subsidiaries to their
parent groups or affiliates grew by 18 percent while imports
grew at 17 percent. The initially faster growth in intra-firm
export trade (1964–1969) was compensated for by the relatively faster import (foreign purchases) growth rate in the
1972 to 1981 period (15 percent for purchases and 13 percent for sales) which reduced the benefit to Canada's balance of trade.

The great degree of intra-firm (U.S. parent-subsidiary)
trade relative to intra-industry trade can be seen in table
3.4. This table reports the ratio of sales (M_p) and purchases
(X_p) by the U.S. parent groups, to all foreign purchases (M)
and sales (X) by the U.S.-owned affiliates in Canada. The
vast majority of trade is intra-firm. From 1964 to 1981 the
U.S. affiliates imported 70 percent and exported 69 percent,
on average, of all their foreign purchases and sales to and
from their parent corporations in the United States. The
trend with sales appears to have increased, since between
1977 and 1982, sales to the parent groups accounted for 73
percent of all foreign sales by the U.S. subsidiaries. The relative importance of purchases from the U.S. parents appears to have increased; from the low 60 to mid-70 percent
range of total foreign purchases in the late 1960s and early
1970s, to an average of 72 percent since 1969. This would
confirm the observations from table 3.3, that sales to the
U.S. parent groups from the Canadian subsidiaries (exports)
grew slower than did purchases (imports) by U.S. subsidiaries from their parent groups.

The extremely high degree of intra-firm trade, reflected
in both sales and purchases, is due to the high degree of
integration between U.S. subsidiary corporations and their
parent groups. This leads to one of the important conclusions of this study, namely, that the U.S. parent groups are

viewing the United States-Canada market as an integrated market area. They plan their subsidiary production within this larger framework. These data undermine the notion that U.S. subsidiaries in Canada are purely branch plants, as argued by the "tariff factory" theory of production. In many cases these tariffs have been lowered or removed over the last fifteen years, in accordance with the seven rounds of GATT trade liberalization. Today, however, there are non-tariff barriers to trade, but their impact on the decisions of where to locate affiliates is more complex than the branch plant argument.

Finally, a ratio is presented in table 3.5 to illustrate further the high degree of intra-firm trade. Table 3.5 reports the balance-of-trade of the affiliates sales to the parents (X_p) as a percentage of the affiliates total purchases from the parent groups (M_p). In the 1979 to 1981 period, this index has averaged 91 percent. This, however, is below the average from 1964 to 1981 of 97.66 percent. Therefore, over the long term, intra-firm trade appears to have been approximately balanced, with the subsidiaries shipping nearly as much back to their parents as they have been purchasing from them.

To summarize, these data confirm the two key observations made with reference to tables 3.2 and 3.3. First, U.S. subsidiaries in Canada tend to import slightly more than they export, however, trade is relatively balanced. Second, the deficit in trade (from Canada's point of view), is not due primarily to non-parent or affiliate to subsidiary trade, but is also due to other two-way trade between Canada and the United States and other countries. The five year accumulated "deficit" from table 3.1 is Cdn. $5,056 million for foreign sales and purchases of all U.S. subsidiaries, but it is only Cdn. $3,550 million for their intra-firm trade as indicated by table 3.3. Overall, the data in tables 3.1 to 3.5 provide strong confirmation for the conclusion that U.S. subsidiaries in Canada do more than just produce for the Canadian market; they also contribute in a major way to Canadian exports. This pattern of bilateral trade demonstrates that U.S. parent groups view the United States-Canada market as an integrated market and plan their investment and production decisions accordingly.

Table 3.5

Intra-Firm Trade for U.S. Subsidiaries in Canada

Year	Ratio of Total Sales to Total Purchases by U.S. Subsidiaries with their Parent Groups
1981	93.18
1980	92.99
1979	87.70
1978	103.38
1977	102.72
1976	100.09
1975	101.04
1974	97.01
1973	105.08
1972	108.91
1971	115.65
1970	124.94
1969	118.66
1968	111.10
1967	117.19
1966	103.51
1965	77.30
1964	87.38

Sources: Canada, Department of Regional Industrial Expansion, *Foreign-Owned Subsidiaries in Canada: 1979–1981* Ottawa: Surveys and Analysis, Statistical and Data Base Services, DRIE, September, 1984): Tables 1, 8, 13 and 14.

Canada, Department of Industry, Trade and Commerce, *Foreign-Owned Subsidiaries in Canada*, [various years] (Ottawa: Statistical and Data Base Services, IT & C (DRIE), April 1983, May 1975, 1974, August 1972 and 1970): Tables 1, 8, 3, 13, 14, Summary Table 27, Appendix VI and Appendix VIII.

BILATERAL TRADE PERFORMANCE OF CANADIAN-OWNED AFFILIATES

In this section attention is directed towards the trade performance of Canada's multinationals operating in the United States. The analysis is based on the data gathered in the annual surveys by the U.S. Department of Commerce of all foreign affiliates in the United States. In 1984 there were 1,395 Canadian-owned affiliates in the United States identified by the Commerce data. Therefore, this section reviews the extent of intra-firm trade for *all* of the Canadian subsidiaries in the United States, not just the largest 21 studied later in chapter 5. The objective of this section is to investigate the nature of intra-industry and intra-firm trade and the extent to which Canada enjoys a large trade surplus in such trade with its U.S. affiliates.

Table 3.6 presents data on the sales and trade performance of Canada's affiliates in the United States from 1977 to 1984. Column one shows the amount of sales, column two their foreign sales (X), while column three shows the amount of foreign purchases (M) by Canada's subsidiaries in the United States. There is a data break between 1980 and 1981, due to a change in methodology involved in a Commerce Department benchmark survey. This means that the data for 1981 and following years are not directly comparable for 1980 and previous years. In 1984 the total sales by Canadian affiliates in the United States were U.S. $82.5 billion, but their foreign sales were only U.S. $4.5 billion. The vast majority of sales by Canada's multinationals are made within the U.S. market itself; only about 6 percent of production and sales by Canada's affiliates is not made within the United States.

Over the most recent period of data availability (1982 to 1984) the foreign sales by Canada's U.S. affiliates grew by 5 percent per annum. This was only half as fast as the growth of total sales (which includes the small amount of foreign sales) of these affiliates over the same period, which was 11 percent per annum. Foreign sales of the Canadian affiliates slowed down in the 1982 and 1983 periods, from U.S. $4.5 billion in 1981, to U.S. $4.2 billion in 1982, before climbing back in 1983 to nearly the same level as in 1981. Foreign purchases declined by 16 percent from 1981 to 1982 and fell a further 1 percent in the 1982–1983 period before rebounding by 20 percent in 1984, to U.S. $7.2 billion. These temporary reductions in the trade deficits of Canada's U.S. affiliates, over the 1981 to 1984 period, were probably due to the differential impact of the recession. The United States was less affected by the recession than Canada; total sales of Canadian affiliates grew faster (at over 10 percent per annum) from 1981 to 1984, but purchases from their Canadian parents grew slower (at under 1 percent).

Table 3.6

Sales, Foreign Sales and Foreign Purchases by Canadian Affiliates
in the United States (millions U.S. $)

Year	(1) Sales by Canadian Affiliates in the United States	(2) Foreign Sales by Canadian Affiliates in the United States	(3) Foreign Purchases by Canadian Affiliates in the United States	(4) U.S. Balance of Intra-Industry Trade
1984	82,483	4.506	7.213	(2.709)
1983	72,037	4.290	5.995	(1.705)
1982	64,909	4.162	6.071	(1.909)
1981	60,927	4.528	8.223	(3.195)
1980	35,456	1.792	5.553	(3.761)
1979	29,067	1.763	5.194	(3.431)
1978	24,555	1.325	4.664	(3.339)
1977	19,733	854	3.853	(2.999)

Sources: U.S. Department of Commerce, Bureau of Economic Analysis, *Foreign Direct Investment in the United States: Operations of U.S. Affiliates, 1977–80* (Washington, D.C.: 1985): Data for 1977–1980.

U.S. Department of Commerce, Bureau of Economic Analysis, *Foreign Direct Investment in the United States: Annual Survey Results: Revised 1981 Estimates, Revised 1982 Estimates, Revised 1983 Estimates and Preliminary 1984 Estimates* (Washington, D.C.: December 1984, December 1985, October 1986 and October 1986): Data for 1981 through 1984 (from Table G.4).

It is apparent from the data in table 3.6 that Canada's affiliates have consistently purchased more outside the United States ("imported") than they have "exported" from the United States. From the perspective of the U.S. Commerce Department, the data in table 3.6 indicate a negative balance for the United States on the trade of the Canadian affiliates, a form of intra-industry trade. In 1984 they imported U.S. $2.7 billion more than they exported. This has been a consistent pattern since 1977. As will be demonstrated later, most of the imports of Canadian affiliates are from their Canadian parents. This means that, from a Canadian perspective, there is an intra-industry trade surplus with Canada's affiliates in the United States.

Table 3.7 indicates the degree of international involvement of Canada's affiliates in the United States. The foreign sales of Canada's U.S. affiliates are given as a percentage of total sales by these affiliates. In 1984, Canadian affiliates had sales of U.S. $82.5 billion and export sales of $4.5 billion, for a foreign sales to total sales ratio of 5.46 percent. For Canadian multinationals the vast majority of their sales are made basically in the U.S. market. Since 1981 this ratio has been declining, showing that Canada's subsidiaries in the United States are now selling even greater shares of their output in the United States than in other countries. But while the relative amount of foreign sales to total sales is falling, it was already documented in table 3.6, that in absolute terms, the foreign sales of these subsidiaries are still increasing.

Table 3.7 also reports the ratio of foreign purchases for Canadian affiliates in the United States. From 1977 to 1984 foreign purchases to sales of Canada's U.S. subsidiaries have fallen from 19.53 percent in 1977 to 8.74 percent in 1984. This indicates that, in relative terms, foreign purchases have been declining in importance as sources of inputs to Canada's subsidiaries in the United States. Once again, in absolute terms, it is important to keep in mind that the subsidiaries foreign purchases are still increasing, as was shown in table 3.6. However, for 1984 the export ratio of 5.46 percent and the import ratio of 8.74 percent reflect the nearly U.S. $3 billion deficit in trade for the United States by Canada's multinationals. Conversely, since most

Table 3.7

Ratios of Foreign Sales and Foreign Purchases to Total Sales by Canadian
Affiliates in the United States
1977–1984

Year	Foreign Sales by Canadian Affiliates as a Percentage of Total Sales by these Canadian Affiliates (%)	Foreign Purchases by Canadian Affiliates in the United States as a Percentage of Total Sales by these Canadian Affiliates (%)
1984	5.46	8.74
1983	5.96	8.32
1982	6.41	9.35
1981	7.43	13.50
1980	5.05	15.66
1979	6.07	17.87
1978	5.40	18.99
1977	4.33	19.53

Sources: U.S. Department of Commerce, Bureau of Economic Analysis, *Foreign Direct Investment in the United States: Operations of U.S. Affiliates, 1977–80* (Washington, D.C.: 1985): Data for 1977–1980.

U.S. Department of Commerce, Bureau of Economic Analysis, *Foreign Direct Investment in the United States: Annual Survey Results: Revised 1981 Estimates, Revised 1982 Estimates, Revised 1983 Estimates* and *Preliminary 1984 Estimates* (Washington, D.C.: December 1984, December 1985, October 1986 and October 1986): Data for 1981 through 1984 (from Table G.4 and E.5).

of the "imports" are sourced from Canada itself, there is a surplus in Canada's trade with its U.S. affiliates, as confirmed by more precise measures of intra-firm trade (to which we now turn).

Table 3.8 presents data on the sales and purchases between Canada's subsidiaries in the United States and their parent groups in Canada; these are measures of intra-firm trade. Column one shows sales by the Canadian affiliates in the United States to their parent groups (X_p), while column two shows purchases by the Canadian affiliates from their parent groups in Canada (M_p).

As table 3.8 also demonstrates, sales by Canadian affiliates to their parents have been growing at approximately 9 percent since 1982, while purchases have been growing at approximately 7 percent over the same period. Just as the recession appeared to have slowed down *total* purchases by the Canadian subsidiaries in the 1982 and 1983 period (table 3.6), similarly, sales to their affiliates by the parent groups declined from a peak in 1981, of U.S. $5.5 billion, to U.S. $4.2 billion in 1982.

The difference between the intra-firm sales and purchases, is the bilateral balance of intra-firm trade due to activities of Canadian multinationals operating in the United States. Table 3.8 also reveals that Canada enjoys about a U.S. $4 billion surplus in such intra-firm trade. Canadian af-

Table 3.8

Intra-Firm Trade: Sales and Purchases by Canadian Affiliates in the United States to and from their Parent Groups in Canada
(millions U.S. $)

Year	Sales by Canadian Affiliates in the United States to their Parent Groups	Purchases by Canadian Affiliates in the United States from their Parent Groups	Canadian Balance
1984	881	4,847	3,966
1983	811	4,357	3,546
1982	740	4,218	3,478
1981	928	5,462	4,534
1980	953	4,559	3,606
1979	964	4,367	3,403
1978	715	3,903	3,188
1977	454	3,300	2,846

Sources: U.S. Department of Commerce, Bureau of Economic Analysis, *Foreign Direct Investment in the United States: Operations of U.S. Affiliates, 1977–80* (Washington, D.C.: 1985): Data for 1977–1980.

U.S. Department of Commerce, Bureau of Economic Analysis, *Foreign Direct Investment in the United States: Annual Survey Results: Revised 1981 Estimates, Revised 1982 Estimates, Revised 1983 Estimates* and *Preliminary 1984 Estimates* (Washington, D.C.: December 1984, December 1985, October 1986 and October 1986): Data for 1981 through 1984 (from Table G.4).

filiates in the United States purchase about U.S. $4 billion
more from their Canadian parents than they sell back to
them from their U.S. production and distribution facilities.
This trade surplus, from a Canadian perspective, generates
jobs and wealth in Canada, due to the market access
achieved by the presence of these Canadian multinationals
in the United States.

Since 1981, purchases from the parent groups in Canada have been approximately five times the level of sales by
the Canadian affiliates back to their parent groups, averaging a U.S. $4 billion deficit from the U.S. perspective. This is
explained by our theoretical knowledge that the Canadian-
owned affiliates operating in the United States are often relatively new companies that need supplies, components, and
knowhow from their parents. It also reflects the key reason
why these subsidiaries were set up in the first place—to secure access to the United States market. The vast majority
of the sales of these affiliates are in the United States itself;
only a small proportion is exported (under 6 percent in
1984 as discussed previously in table 3.7).

The relative degree of importance of the Canadian parent groups to their Canadian affiliates is also demonstrated
in table 3.9. This table reports the sales and purchases by
the Canadian affiliates in the United States to and from
their parent groups as a percentage of total foreign sales
and purchases. This ratio in 1984 stood at 19.55 percent
and since 1981 has averaged 19.18 percent. Table 3.9 shows
the ratio of purchases by the Canadian affiliates from their
parent groups (M_p) as a percentage of all foreign purchases
(M). In 1984 this ratio stood at 67.20 percent, down from
72.68 percent the year before. Since 1981 the ratio has averaged 68.95 percent. The breaks in the ratio in 1981 are
mainly explained by methodological changes in the Department of Commerce benchmark survey.

Table 3.10 provides the final pieces of additional information about the balance of intra-firm trade between Canada's parent multinationals and their U.S. subsidiaries. This
ratio is an indicator of the degree of sales (exports) by the
affiliates to their parents (X_p), over the affiliates purchases
(imports) from their parents (M_p). With a high ratio, the

Table 3.9

Intra-Firm Trade Ratios
for the Canadian Affiliates in the United States

Year	Sales to the Parent Group as a Percentage of all Foreign Sales	Purchases from the Parent Groups as a Percentage of all Foreign Purchases
	%	%
1984	19.55	67.20
1983	18.90	72.68
1982	17.78	66.48
1981	20.49	69.42
1980	53.18	82.10
1979	54.68	84.08
1978	53.96	83.68
1977	53.16	85.65

Sources: U.S. Department of Commerce, Bureau of Economic Analysis, *Foreign Direct Investment in the United States: Operations of U.S. Affiliates, 1977–80* (Washington, D.C.: 1985): Data for 1977–1980.

U.S. Department of Commerce, Bureau of Economic Analysis, *Foreign Direct Investment in the United States: Annual Survey Results: Revised 1981 Estimates, Revised 1982 Estimates, Revised 1983 Estimates* and *Preliminary 1984 Estimates* (Washington, D.C.: December 1984, December 1985, October 1986 and October 1986): Data for 1981 and 1982 (From Table G.4).

Canadian-owned subsidiaries in the United States would be shipping nearly as many products back to Canada as they are purchasing from their parents. Conversely, from the perspective of Canada's balance of trade, a low ratio means that the affiliates of Canadian multinationals buy more from Canada than they sell back to parent Canadian firms. The ratio of the bilateral intra-firm trade balance is indeed low and it has fallen in recent years. The ratio of bilateral intra-firm trade stood at 18.18 percent for 1984, indicating that the U.S. subsidiaries of Canada's multinationals sell about one-fifth as much to their parents as they import from them. This confirms that Canada runs a surplus on its intra-firm balance of trade with its U.S. subsidiaries. As explained earlier the break in the data set, due to the 1981

Table 3.10

Intra-Firm Trade for Canadian Affiliates in the United States

Year	Ratio of Total Sales to Total Purchases by the Canadian Affiliates with their Parent Groups
1984	18.18
1983	18.61
1982	17.54
1981	16.99
1980	20.90
1979	22.07
1978	18.32
1977	13.76

Sources: U.S. Department of Commerce, Bureau of Economic Analysis, *Foreign Direct Investment in the United States: Operations of U.S. Affiliates, 1977–80* (Washington, D.C. 1985): Data for 1977–1980.

U.S. Department of Commerce, Bureau of Economic Analysis, *Foreign Direct Investment in the United States: Annual Survey Results: Revised 1981 Estimates, Revised 1982 Estimates, Revised 1983 Estimates* and Preliminary 1984 Estimates (Washington, D.C.: December 1984, December 1985, October 1986 and October 1986): Data for 1981 through 1984 (from Table G.4).

Commerce benchmark survey, is the primary reason for the great difference in the ratios over the two distinct periods, 1977–1980 and 1981–1984.

CONCLUSIONS

Bilateral patterns of foreign direct investment are a double-edged sword. This chapter has demonstrated that Canadian multinationals play an important role in helping Canada to benefit from its foreign direct investment in the United States. Over the last ten years they have substantially increased their stake in the United States. This has resulted in a benefit to Canada since Canada's affiliates purchase five times as much from Canada as they ship back to Canada. This may gradually change as the firms in the United States mature and become self-reliant. However, over the forseeable future, the reliance of the affiliates on Canadian inputs is likely to continue. Further discussion of the factors that will affect the decisions of these firms, can be found in chapter 6 where the effects of bilateral trade and strategic management are considered.

On the other edge of the sword it has been shown that the more mature U.S. subsidiaries in Canada for the last 20 years have purchased roughly the same amount from the United States, in most cases from their parent groups, as they sell back to them. This evidence dismisses the belief that all U.S. subsidiaries are still just branch plant factories in the Canadian economy.

An implication of the two findings is that adjustment following bilateral trade liberalization will be more involved than the common perception that U.S. subsidiaries will be closing down their plants and going home. Many of the U.S. operations in Canada form part of a larger, strategically integrated network of companies. These companies in many cases have large sums of capital tied up in production facilities, human capital, marketing, and distribution networks. While some part of these capital investments may be explained by tariffs or even non-tariff barriers, a large number of them are determined by competitive market conditions. These issues are discussed in more detail beginning in chapter 5. However, the next chapter extends the analysis of this one by considering the costs and benefits of bilateral direct investments.

NOTE TO CHAPTER 3

As is well known, about one-third of bilateral trade is already liberalized through the auto pact. This is a managed trade agreement which permits the largest three U.S. multinational auto producers to assemble autos without being subject to tariffs, provided safeguards for Canadian content in output and employment are met. In practice the proportions of Canadian content are easily met and the safeguards have not been required.

The data in table 3.2 can be adjusted to exclude trade in autos (cars and trucks). For example, in 1977 a foreign sales ratio of 26.35 percent was calculated for all U.S. subsidiaries in Canada. If the auto trade is excluded this ratio is approximately 16 percent. The ratios for the succeeding years,

1978 to 1981 are as follows: 16.01, 16.22, 14.75, and 13.72. Using a slightly different data set the ratios for 1982 to 1984 are: 14.56, 13.50, and 18.84.

It can also be noted at this time that the data in table 5.2 on the top 19 industrial U.S. subsidiaries in Canada can be adjusted. The average exports to sales ratios for all firms is 36 percent; without the three auto makers it is 22 percent. This figure is very similar to the aggregate data presented in table 3.2 for foreign sales, and the adjusted data quoted above. Hence, none of the conclusions offered are affected by this adjustment. Finally the obvious caveat should be made: It is scientifically unjustified to exclude the auto pact trade from these data. A false picture is created when this is done. The U.S. auto multinationals are an inescapable component of bilateral trade and investments and they are an integral part of the data sets reported and analyzed in this study.

Chapter 4

The Benefits to Canada of Multinational Enterprises

This chapter combines the data introduced in the previous chapter to evaluate the benefits and costs to Canada of foreign direct investment. First, the bilateral balance of trade, due to intra-firm trade, is found. This involves finding the deficit incurred by Canada on the net purchases of U.S.-owned subsidiaries in Canada and comparing it with the net surplus on purchases from Canada by Canadian-owned affiliates in the United States. These data are adjusted into Canadian dollars. It is found that there is a net surplus to Canada on the intra-firm trade of these two types of multinationals. Next, the high degree of integration of the United States and Canadian economies is further demonstrated by estimation of the bilateral index of the national balance in trade and production and this is compared to the experience of European nations and Japan. Finally the data on intra-firm trade are used as a basis to evaluate the employment-related aspects of adjustment to trade liberalization. Again it is found that Canada benefits from the jobs secured by multinational enterprises (mainly from the manner in which Canadian-owned multinationals generate jobs by their sales in the United States) and that trade liberalization will probably enhance such benefits.

CANADA'S TRADE SURPLUS DUE TO MULTINATIONAL ENTERPRISES

Using the information from chapter 3 it is possible to determine the net balance of trade for Canada from the activity of multinational enterprises. This requires that the net trade performance of U.S. subsidiaries in Canada be compared with that of Canadian-owned affiliates in the United States. As demonstrated in chapter 3 there is a net deficit on the trade of the former and a net surplus (from Canada's perspective) on the latter.

Table 4.1 reports the data on Canada's balance of trade for multinational enterprises. Actual data for column 1 on the balance of trade for U.S. subsidiaries in Canada are available only until 1981. The data for 1982–1984 are projections, based on extrapolated averages of the sales and purchases of these subsidiaries over previous periods, as explained in the Appendix to chapter 4.

Table 4.1

Canada's Balance of Intra-Firm Trade
(millions C$)

	Sales Less Purchases by U.S. Subsidiaries in Canada to their Parents	Purchases Less Sales by Canadian affiliates in the United States to their Parents	Net Balance
1984	(2210) b	5241	3031
1983	(1596) b	4413	2817
1982	(1197) b	4276	3079
1981	(1071)	5377	4306
1980	(1006)	4308	3302
1979	(1924)	3975	2051
1978	451	3781	4232
1977	310	3115	3425
1976	9	2789c	2798
1975	83	2724c	2807

Notes: (a) Column 2 is derived from Commerce data in U.S. $ multiplied by the year end exchange rate to convert the data to Cdn. $. For example the 1981 exchange rate was 1.1859.

    (b) Data for 1982, 1983, and 1984 are the extrapolated averages for sales and for purchases, based on the mean of the averages of their immediate past 5 and 16 years growth.

    (c) Data for 1976 and 1975 are extrapolated from averages for sales and for purchases, based on the mean of the average sales from 1981 to 1984.

Sources: Canada, Department of Regional Industrial Expansion *Foreign-Owned Subsidiaries in Canada: 1979–1981* (Ottawa: Survey and Analysis, Statistical and Data Base Surveys, DRIE, September 1984): Table 13.

Canada, Department of Industry, Trade and Commerce/Regional Economic Expansion, *Foreign-Owned Subsidiaries in Canada: 1973–1979* (Ottawa: Surveys and Analysis, Statistical and Data Base Services, I T & C and DRIE, April 1983): Table 13.

Building on tables 3.3 and 3.8 for 1981, the last year for observable data, Canada's trade deficit on the intra-firm trade of its U.S. subsidiaries was just over Cdn. $1 billion, as shown in column 1 of table 4.1. This is due to the foreign purchases of U.S. subsidiaries in Canada being greater than their sales. However, as column 2 reveals, in 1981 there was a larger trade surplus of over Cdn. $5.3 billion, due to the purchases of Canadian-owned affiliates in the United States from their parent groups being much greater than the sales back to their parents. Therefore, Canada's net balance of trade surplus on multinational enterprise activity, for 1981 was Cdn. $4.3 billion.

In more recent years Canada's projected intra-firm trade balance has also been positive, due to the continued surplus generated by Canadian-owned subsidiaries, as shown by the actual data in column 2. Even if the projected data for 1982–1984 on U.S. subsidiaries in Canada are subject to error it is highly unlikely that the pattern of the persistent trade surplus indicated in column 3 would be reversed. The conclusion is inescapable: Canada enjoys a large and stable trade surplus due to the presence of multinational enterprises in its economy. The development of Canadian-owned multinationals has led to growing trade surpluses as their U.S. affiliates purchase much more from Canada than they sell to Canada. These huge surpluses offset the relatively small trade deficits incurred by U.S.-owned subsidiaries in Canada. From table 4.1 the average trade surplus for Canada over the 1981–1984 period was Cdn. $3.3 billion, while for the 1975–1980 period it was Cdn. $2.8 billion. The average trade surplus over the 10 years, from 1975 to 1984, was $3.1 billion. A word of caution on this figure is necessary, however, due to the Department of Commerce data break between 1980 and 1981. Because of this data break the $3.1 billion surplus should be regarded as indicative of the pat tern of trade but not the average absolute figure for the balance of trade. The Appendix to this chapter goes beyond intra-firm trade and provides more detailed information on the costs to Canada of U.S. subsidiaries compared to the benefits of Canadian affiliates in the United States.

The implications of this finding are only just beginning to be appreciated. They include recognition of the economic

benefits of multinational activity, including beneficial employment effects. The net trade surplus also suggests that
adjustment problems due to trade liberalization could be
resolved to Canada's benefit given the key role played by
Canadian-owned multinationals in generating the bilateral
intra-industry trade surplus.

NATIONAL BALANCE IN TRADE AND PRODUCTION

Before considering the national balance in trade and
production between two nations it is useful to first review
the concept of intra-industry trade. Intra-industry trade is
defined as two-way trade flows in the same sector. The classic measure of intra-industry trade was developed by Grubel
and Lloyd (1975). It can be calculated for an industry (i) as:

$$IIT_i = [(X_i + M_i) - X_i - M_i / (X_i + M_i)]$$

where IIT_i = index of intra-industry trade for industry i
         X_i = exports from industry i
         M_i = imports of industry i

MacCharles (1985a, 1987) has made calculations of IIT
at the industry level for 159 industries in Canada, although
he does not report a direct figure for an aggregate IIT index.
Using the Grubel and Lloyd index, Cantwell (1986) reports
the level of IIT for some countries as: United States, 0.70;
France, 0.85; West Germany, 0.71; Italy, 0.86; and the United
Kingdom, 0.83.

The significance of the index of intra-industry trade is
that if the index is 1.0 for a nation, then all of its trade is in
the form of two-way flows. This means that there is no apparent comparative advantage in the traditional Heckscher-
Ohlin-Samuelson sense. With an IIT index of 1.0 the nation
does not export and import certain categories of products
according to its relative factor endowments; instead it
trades everything across the board. This appears to be the
case of European nations as well as for the United States
and Canada. In contrast, Cantwell reports the IIT index as
0.60 for Japan, which indicates that Japanese trade is less
intra-industry and that the range of imported goods differs
from exports.

Previous work has demonstrated a close relationship
between intra-industry trade and international production

(foreign direct investment), see Dunning (1981), Helleiner (1981), Rugman (1985b), Helpman and Krugman (1985) Greenaway and Tharakan (1986), and Casson et al. (1986), etc. All of these authors have identified multinational enterprises as key components of both intra-industry trade and intra-industry production. Most of these authors have demonstrated a high correlation between intra-industry trade and production. In similar industries (like automobiles, chemicals, or metals) there will be cross-investments by multinational enterprises and a high level of intra-industry trade. However, there are exceptions. For example, a country that is a poor location for R & D and technological innovation may have a low index of intra-industry trade (as low exports would be accompanied by high imports of the product) but a high index of intra-industry production (since there would be neither outward nor inward foreign direct investment because multinationals would scorn the country), which we will discuss next.

It is also possible to calculate an index of intra-industry production, or as some authors such as Erdilek (1985) would call it, an index of intra-industry foreign direct investment. By either term is meant the production made by firms from two different countries but from the same industry. Obviously this type of production is undertaken by multinational enterprises, (defined as firms producing abroad). Examples occur in the automobile industry, pharmaceutical industry, and cement industry, where production takes place in both the United States and Canada by multinational enterprises. Indeed, the great bulk of bilateral trade is now in the form of intra-industry production, reflecting the increasing economic and financial integration of the United States and Canada. Even in resource-based industries such as pulp and paper, fish products, and minerals there is now a large degree of intra-industry production, by both U.S. and Canadian-owned multinationals in each other's markets.

The index of intra-industry production is calculated as follows:

$$IIP_i = \frac{[(OP_i + IP_i) - |OP_i - IP_i|]}{(OP_i + IP_i)}$$

where IIP_i = index of intra-industry production
   OP_i = outward international production of the firms
         in country i
   IP_i = inward international production of the
         foreign-owned subsidiaries of country i

   An index of the national balance of production will be conceptually similar to an index of intra-industry production but it looks at the foreign production in aggregate rather than at the industry level. A bilateral balance of production can also be developed by looking at the foreign production between two countries only. Empirical evidence on the high degree of national balance of production is displayed in column 1 of table 4.2 Building upon the work of Cantwell (1986, 1987) it can be observed that the index of the bilateral balance of production for Canada and the United States is 0.74. The U.S. index against all other countries in 1982, is 0.69.

   To calculate Canada's index of bilateral balance of production, data on OP_i were found from the U.S. Department of Commerce survey on the sales of all Canadian-owned affiliates in the United States, while data on IP_i were found from the CALURA data on the sales by U.S.-owned subsidiaries in Canada, both for 1982. This procedure was repeated for the years 1977 to 1983 and the results are shown in column 2, table 4.2. The index for 1983, at 0.78, reveals an increase over earlier years. The average ratio from 1981 to 1983 is 0.74 and from 1977 to 1980 is 0.46. This is partly accounted for by an increase in affiliates reporting after a change in methodology in the U.S. Department of Commerce Benchmark Survey of 1980.

   What is the meaning of the index of the bilateral balance of production? For Canada, inward international production (IP_i) is greater than outward international production (OP_i). This reflects the greater stock of U.S. foreign direct investment in Canada than Canadian foreign direct investment in the United States. The U.S.-owned subsidiaries in Canada had sales of Cdn. $139.5 billion in 1983 (or U.S. $112.1 billion, converting at the IMF year-end market exchange rate of 1.2444). The sales of Canadian-owned subsidiaries for

Table 4.2

Index of National Balance of Production

Index of the National Balance of Production 1982		Index of Bilateral Balance of Production	
Canada (a)	0.74	1983	0.78
United States	0.69	1982	0.74
France	0.88	1981	0.71
West Germany	0.79	1980	0.49
Italy	0.65	1979	0.48
United Kingdom	0.60	1978	0.46
Japan	0.38	1977	0.40

Note: (a) Bilateral production only, calculated by the author using Cantwell's methodology.

Sources: John A. Cantwell "Technological Competition and Intra-Industry Production in Europe," paper to the European International Business Association, London, November 1986. See also John A. Cantwell: *Technological Innovation and Multinational Corporations* (Oxford: Basil Blackwell, 1987).

U.S. Department of Commerce, Bureau of Economic Analysis, *Foreign Direct Investment in the United States: Operations of U.S. Affiliates, 1977–80* (Washington, D.C.: 1985): Data for 1977–1980.

U.S. Department of Commerce, Bureau of Economic Analysis, *Foreign Direct Investment in the United States: Annual Survey Results: Revised 1981 Estimates, Revised 1982 Estimates, Revised 1983 Results* and *Preliminary 1984 Results* (Washington D.C.: December 1984, December 1985, October 1986 and October 1986): Data for 1981 through 1981 (from Table G.4).

Canada, Statistics Canada, *Corporations and Labour Unions Returns Act: Part 1 Corporations*, Ottawa: Supply and Services Canada, Catalogue 61–210, 1978–1983): Table 4.

1983 were U.S. $72 billion, roughly half the value of the older and more established U.S. subsidiaries in Canada.

If the index of bilateral balance of production were 1.0 it would mean that Canadian outward investment and international production would exactly balance U.S. inward investment and international production in Canada. This will not occur for a few more years, until the newer stock of Canadian direct investment in the United States leads to sufficient sales by Canadian-owned subsidiaries to match the large output of U.S.-owned subsidiaries in Canada.

Many of the European nations have similar large ratios of the national balance of production, namely France, Germany, Italy, and the United Kingdom, see table 4.2. On the other hand the index for Japan is only 0.38 for 1982, reflecting the relative lack of inward investment in Japan.

If the index of national balance of production is zero, it means that the nation only has outward direct investment and is host to no foreign subsidiaries. It is difficult to conceive of any nation that could achieve such a result in today's interdependent global economic system. Indeed, a zero index of the national balance of production would be of questionable benefit in any case, since it would probably reflect a strongly regulated economy and one suffering from a high degree of political risk, at least as perceived by foreign direct investors. There would be no jobs created by inward investment and it is to be expected that national income and economic efficiency would be low in such an economy (with the notable exception of Japan).

There are several theories advanced to explain the spread of international production. Cantwell (1986) suggests that multinationals engage in technological competition, seeking to establish both R & D and production methods across key nations in which technological innovation is favoured. To remain competitive with other multinational enterprises in the same industry (e.g., pharmaceutical) European multinationals seek to produce in the domestic locations of competitors whose home country characteristics have provided conducive environments for R & D and technological advance. Consequently, attractive locations for technological innovation will generate a high index of the national balance of production. Paradoxically very unattractive locations could also score a high index, since there will then be little outward or inward direct investment.

Extending this line of thinking to update the product cycle model of Vernon (1966) would imply that innovative nations such as the United States, which Vernon saw as home nation for world-wide outward direct investment, are now also host nations for inward direct investments by rivals.

Hymer (1976) had a similar vision of the world, but couched his analysis in the unduly restrictive terms of oligopolistic rivalry, in which multinational enterprises were assumed to have monopolistic assets on which rents were earned. Yet when we observe cross-investments (to the extent that the United States is today simultaneously the world's largest host and home nation for foreign direct investment) then it is unlikely that any rents remain for very long. The multinational enterprises from Europe, the United States, Canada, and third world countries compete with each other for a share of the global market and segments of markets, which yields only normal profits over time (Rugman, Lecraw, and Booth 1985, chapter 6).

BENEFITS AND COSTS OF CANADIAN OUTWARD INVESTMENT

Due to the critical importance of Canadian outward direct investment in generating a trade surplus for Canada on its trade by multinational enterprises, this section will explore in more detail the phenomenon of Canadian multinationals. What are the social benefits and costs to Canada of such outward direct investment? To what extent does this condition how Canada's multinationals might adjust to trade liberalization? What are the actual numbers on employment and trade-related aspects of such outward direct investment, especially in the performance of affiliates in the United States?

It is not necessary in this book to undertake a comprehensive analysis of the economic benefits and costs of Canadian outward direct investment. All that is necessary is to realize that analysis of the benefits and costs of foreign direct investment from Canada should recognize the extent of Canada's affiliates in the United States.

The application of simple economic theory, based on MacDougall (1960), would suggest that Canada, as a net capital exporter of foreign direct investment, would suffer a "social" loss of tax receipts. The affiliates of Canadian multinationals operating in the United States would pay U.S. state and federal corporate taxes; Canada would not be able to tax affiliate profits again without subjecting the multinationals to double taxation. As Canada's multinationals are a relatively new event, the Canadian tax authorities have not yet had much experience with such tax credits, especially in contrast to the U.S. tax authorities when they deal with U.S. multinationals operating in Canada.

Besides the tax issue there are other consequences of Canadian outward investment. Based on the premises of internalization theory, discussed earlier, there should be some spreading of external economies to the United States from Canada's multinationals (the other side of the coin of technology transfer by U.S. subsidiaries in Canada). While Canadian multinationals typically are not knowledge or technology-intensive there is still some diffusion of whatever knowhow they possess. This social externality is likely to be of greatest advantage to the U.S. economy through the diffusion of marketing-type skills which are the firm specific advantages of most of the Canadian multinationals. Lest it be thought that Canada is being overly generous to its rich neighbour, it is as well to remember that most of these Canadian multinationals would quite happily contribute to a similar transfer of technology, but through the modality of exporting from Canada, if only U.S. markets were open. Thus, the issue of external economies is not confined to outward investment; it arises when there is any international exchange, including the first best option of free trade.

Globerman (1985) has drawn two similar normative implications about Canadian foreign direct investment. First, he suggests that such outward investment is beneficial since it helps to spread the strengths of Canadian firms over larger markets. If such firm-specific advantages were generated by research and development expenditures (as with Northern Telecom) these overheads can be spread over a larger volume of sales. Building on Rugman and McIlveen (1985) it could also be shown that if the firm-specific advantages were of a more intangible type, embodied in management or marketing skills, then these can be spread on a wider base by Canadian direct investment. Second, Globerman argues that foreign direct investment is complementary to exporting, that is, it does not displace exports. The reason for this conclusion is that exports are denied by tariff and non-tariff barriers to trade, such that a Canadian firm would lose its market unless direct investment were to reopen the foreign market. This argument could be extended to jobs. Outward investment involves some transfer of jobs from Canada to the U.S. plants. However, the jobs in Canada would have been at risk anyway once exporting was denied to the Canadian firm. Eventually outward investment retains market access. It then contributes to Canada's welfare once profits are remitted back to Canada, stimulating Canada's wealth and demand for labour in an indirect manner.

Given these caveats, it is useful here to quickly outline some of the more interesting aspects of the rise in Canadian direct investment in the United States. According to the annual survey of affiliates conducted by the U.S. Department of Commerce, in 1984 Canada had a total of 1,395 affiliates in the United States with total sales of nearly U.S. $82 billion. These firms employed over half a million U.S. workers and they spent over U.S. $14 billion on employee compensation. This is about the same number as Canadians working in U.S. subsidiaries in Canada (see tables 4.3 and 4.4). To keep this in perspective, the total number of employees in Canada's U.S. affiliates is about 5 percent of total employment in Canada. These, and other selected economic data on the affiliates are presented in table 4.3. The table shows both the absolute value of the selected economic data on the affiliates and also their percentage contribution to all the other countries' affiliate activity in the United States.

Although Canada's share of all world direct investment in the United States has been falling in recent years, to about 9 percent of the total by 1984, its large and growing stock of existing direct investment is socially beneficial to the United States and Canada. For example, according to the Commerce data, Canadian affiliates do nearly 30 percent of all the R & D by foreign multinationals in the United States, despite being in mature and resource-based sectors. In terms of jobs, Canadian direct investment accounts for nearly one-fifth of U.S. workers employed in all foreign-owned affiliates. The employment associated with Canadian direct investment is not a social loss to Canada since such jobs would not have existed in any case had the Canadian-owned multinationals not secured access to the U.S. mar-

Table 4.3

Canadian Affiliates in the United States Selected Economic Data, 1984

	U.S. $M 1984	% of all affiliates in the United States 1984
Total Assets	105,392	17.7
Sales	82,483	13.8
Net Income	2,659	28.3
Employee Compensation	14,469	19.8
Number of Employees	505,232	18.6
Land Owned (thousands of acres)	4,732	35.7
Gross book value of property, plant and equipment	64,150	23.9
Expenditure for plant property and equipment	7,764	23.6
U.S. exports shipped by affiliates	4,506	8.0
U.S. imports shipped to affiliates	7,213	7.2
Income taxes	1,385	16.2
R & D expenditures	1,404	29.7

Source: United States Department of Commerce, Bureau of Economic Analysis, *Foreign Direct Investment in the United States Annual Survey Results: Preliminary 1984 Estimates* (Washington D.C., October 1986): Various Tables.

ket. Again, from Canada's viewpoint, the dividends, royalties and fees earned on Canadian direct investment in the United States over the 1984–1985 period were about 5 percent of its stock, and the return was over U.S. $1 billion in 1983 alone. Thus the benefits to Canada from direct investment are underlined by the data in chapter 3, and the conclusion in table 4.1. These data indicate that Canada enjoys a surplus of intra-firm trade with the United States.

The conclusion of ths preliminary excursion into the issue of benefits and costs of Canadian direct investment in the United States should be one of caution. It appears that the Canadian affiliates in the United States employ some half a million workers, have sales of about Cdn. $100 billion, purchase a much larger proportion of goods and services from their Canadian parent firms than they re-export to Canada, and remit some $1 billion in dividends. Such activities complement Canadian production and help Canada to secure access to the U.S. market by foreign direct invest-

Table 4.4

Bilateral Employment in U.S. and Canadian Subsidiaries
in Mining, Manufacturing and Logging Industries

Year	Employment in U.S. Subsidiaries in Canada (a)	Employment in Canadian Affiliates in the United States	Ratio U.S. Subsidiaries/ Canadian Affiliates %
1984	N/A	505,232	N/A
1983	N/A	473,467	N/A
1982	N/A	455,392	N/A
1981	567,461	437,393	129.73
1980	590,591	290,018	203.63
1979	N/A	255,542	N/A
1978	619,454	221,179	280.07
1977	N/A	189,263	N/A
1976	628,340	N/A	N/A
1975	N/A	N/A	N/A
1974	662,802	N/A	N/A

Notes: N/A = Not Available
(a) Manufacturing, mining and logging industries

Sources: Canada, Statistics Canada, *Domestic and Foreign Control of Manufacturing, Mining and Logging Establishments in Canada: 1981* (Ottawa: Supply and Services Canada, Catalogue No. 31–401, July 1985): Table 2, pp. 37–40

U.S. Department of Commerce, Bureau of Economic Analysis, *Foreign Direct Investment in the United States: Operations of U.S. Affiliates, 1977–80* (Washington, D.C.: 1985): Data for 1977–1980 from Table 8.

U.S. Department of Commerce, Bureau of Economic Analysis, *Foreign Direct Investment in the United States: Annual Survey Results: Revised 1981 Estimates, Revised 1982 Estimates, Revised 1983 Results* and *Preliminary 1984 Results* (Washington, D.C.: December 1984, December 1985, October 1986 and October 1986): Data for 1981 through 1981 (from Tables 8 and 8A).

ment. But jobs and sales are not lost to Canada since the U.S. affiliates of Canada's multinationals have kept open access to the U.S. market in the face of U.S. protectionism.

Once the forces of protectionism dictate that international production must replace exporting, then the jobs associated with Canadian exporting fade away and cannot be maintained on the grounds of long-run efficiency. Canadian multinationals are the messengers who signal the news of a more complex global trading environment. Ultimately, evaluation of national benefits and costs is a narrow exercise since there is relatively little that a small open trading economy such as Canada can do to insulate itself from such protectionist trends in world trade and investment patterns. Perhaps through the process of trade liberalization, especially bilateral, this tendency towards outward direct investment can be slowed down. But for the reasons discussed in chapters 5 and 6, it is unlikely to be reversed.

EMPLOYMENT ASPECTS OF BILATERAL TRADE LIBERALIZATION

The logic of the work reported so far indicates that trade liberalization will have relatively little disruptive effect on the employment in multinational enterprises. Already both U.S. subsidiaries in Canada and the newer Canadian affiliates in the United States are engaged in substantial amounts of foreign production and intra-firm trade. They are operating as vehicles for the international exchange of goods and services embodied in their product lines and they are achieving market access through direct investment rather than exporting. Trade liberalization will simply help to smooth out the process of economic integration already accounted for by the foreign production and intra-firm trade of these two sets of multinational enterprises. In this section the extent of employment in multinational enterprises is specifically considered.

In the long run, trade liberalization will ensure gains from trade due to the benefits of economic specialization and the increased opportunities for managers to arrange efficient bilateral exchange, whether in the form of exports, direct investment or non-equity forms of involvement. In all three cases the workers employed by multinational enterprises will benefit from a more secure trading environment and the associated stabilization of the investment climate. Two-way flows of trade and investment will be determined on the basis of optimum economic conditions, to the mutual advantage of the worker and consumer in both Canada and the United States.

It is difficult to acquire data on the employment in U.S. subsidiaries in Canada on a comparable basis to that of employment in the Canadian affiliates in the United States. For example, CALURA does not report this, so other sources were used. From Commerce data the number of employees in Canadian affiliates in the United States in 1984 was 505,232 and 437,393 in 1981. In 1981 there were 567,461 workers in the manufacturing, mining, and logging industries of U.S. subsidiaries in Canada, according to information published in *Domestic and Foreign Control of Manufacturing, Mining and Logging Establishments in Canada: 1981,* by Statistics Canada (July, 1985). This publication understates the number of workers in U.S. subsidiaries since the subsidiaries operate across more than these three sectors.

Comparable data gathered by the U.S. Department of Commerce, and published in *U.S. Direct Investment Abroad: 1982 Benchmark Survey Data,* indicates that in 1982 (there are no figures available for 1981) there were 780,600 Canadians employed by U.S. subsidiaries in Canada. U.S. subsidiary employees in 1981, therefore, in the manufacturing, mining, and logging industries accounted for, approximately, 73 percent of the total employees reported for 1982 in the U.S. Department of Commerce survey. With this qualification table 4.4 reports data on bilateral employment in these two sets of multinationals.

Table 4.4 reports the employment in U.S.-owned subsidiaries in the manufacturing, mining, and logging industries in Canada in 1981. It was about 130 percent of the total of Americans employed in all Canadian affiliates in the United States. Also for 1981 the average shipment (sales) per worker in U.S. subsidiaries was about Cdn. $130,000 in the same industries, whereas the average shipments per worker in similar Canadian-owned domestic corporations was about Cdn. $90,000. This indicates that U.S.-owned subsidiaries in Canada have about 42 percent higher "productivity" (output and sales per worker) than Canadian-owned firms. This ratio has been relatively constant since at least 1970. These "Canadian-owned" firms are domestic Canadian corporations engaged in these industries, including both Canadian-owned multinational enterprises and

Canadian-owned non-multinationals (but not U.S. or other foreign-owned multinationals), as reported in the Statistics Canada data on the manufacturing, mining, and logging industries.

This would confirm earlier observations about the efficiency of these U.S. subsidiaries and the beneficial impact for Canada in the presence of such successful world-class firms. The Canadian economy also benefits from the foreign operation of its multinationals, especially as dividends and other aspects of wealth are remitted back to Canada. There is also a surplus in intra-firm trade, as reported earlier in this chapter. Finally, we notice that foreign-owned subsidiaries in Canada are more efficient and have higher per-worker "productivity" than domestic Canadian corporations, a finding noted over 20 years ago by Safarian (1966).

Canada's Bilateral Balance of Intra-Industry Trade

In this appendix the benefits to Canada of the trade of U.S. subsidiaries in Canada, and the trade of Canadian affiliates in the United States, are discussed in detail. This appendix traces the process of creation of the net benefit of intra-industry and other trade reported in this text and it also supplements the information in table 4.1 in the text. Also discussed is the methodology for making extrapolations for 1982 to 1984 from the Department of Regional Industrial Expansion (DRIE) data and for the U.S. Department of Commerce data from 1975 to 1976. Included is a discussion of the validity of the DRIE data source. It is important to note the definition of intra-industry trade used here (which is the same as in chapter 3). Since all the data reported here are at the aggregate level, intra-industry trade is defined as trade between subsidiaries and all firms in their home countries. Intra-firm trade is defined more narrowly as trade between subsidiaries and their parent groups.

In order to gain a better appreciation of the benefits and costs of intra-industry trade and other trade, it is first useful to observe this in diagrammatic form. This has been done in figure A4.1. Figure A4.1 demonstrates the flows originating between the U.S. subsidiaries and their parent groups on the left, while on the right it shows the flows between the Canadian parent groups and their affiliates in the United States.

From figure A4.1 it may be noticed that U.S. subsidiaries in Canada provide two "benefits" to Canada. First, they export goods, both to the United States (flow 1), including their own parent corporations, and second, to other foreign countries (flow 2). Canada also receives a benefit from having affiliates in the United States, since these affiliates purchase goods from their Canadian parent groups (flow 3).

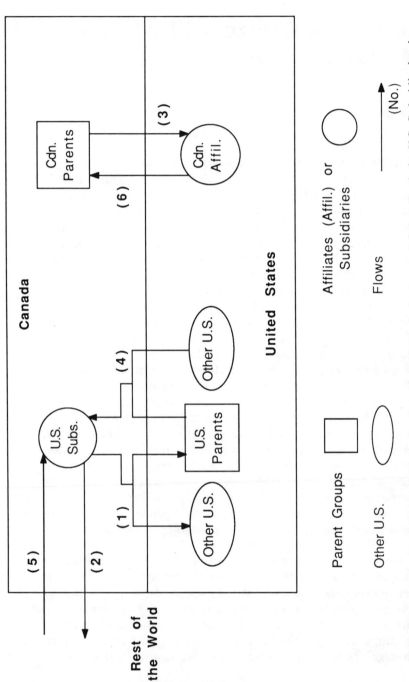

Figure A4.1   The Benefits and Costs for Canada of Intra-Industry and Other Trade by U.S. Subsidiaries in Canada and Canada's Affiliates in the United States

Deducted from these total benefits to Canada are the "costs" of having U.S. subsidiaries in Canada and Canadian multinational affiliates in the United States. Two costs of the U.S. subsidiaries in Canada are: (1) the purchase of goods from their parent groups and other companies in the United States (flow 4), and (2) the purchase of goods from other foreign countries (flow 5). Canadian affiliates in the United States also have a cost for Canada, since Canada's parent groups purchase goods back from their affiliates (flow 6).

A balance sheet of these "flows" for 1984 is carried out in table A4.1. The flow numbers indicated in figure A4.1 are numbered down the left-hand side of table A4.1. From table A4.1 it can be seen that the U.S. subsidiaries in Canada provided a benefit of Cdn. $28,238 million, due to their sales outside of Canada (flow 1 and 2), while Canadian subsidiaries provided a benefit of Cdn. $6,405 million, due to their purchases from their Canadian parent groups (flow 3). This provided a total benefit to Canada of Cdn. $34,643 million in 1984.

The U.S. subsidiaries, however, cost Canada Cdn. $32,451 million, due to their purchases from outside of Canada (flows 4 and 5). The Canadian parent groups also purchased goods back from their affiliates, which further reduced the benefits to Canada by Cdn. $1,164 million (flow 6). This amount is, however, only 3.6 percent of the U.S. subsidiaries purchases from all foreign countries, including the United States.

After deducting all the costs to Canada of the U.S. subsidiaries and Canadian affiliates, Canada had a net benefit in its subsidiary-affiliate balance of bilateral trade of Cdn. $1,029 million in 1984. For reasons discussed later, this may even underestimate the amount of Canada's bilateral trade surplus of the U.S. subsidiaries in Canada and Canada's affiliates in the United States.

A similar analysis can be carried out for the other years, from 1975 to 1983, as these data are also presented in tables A4.2 to A4.6. The final table, table A4.6, indicates a positive net benefit to Canada of having U.S. subsidiaries in Canada, and of Canada operating its own affiliates in the United States. From 1981 to 1984 the average net benefit to

Table A4.1

Net Bilateral Balance of Trade by U.S. Subsidiaries
in Canada and Canada's Affiliates
in the United States (1984) (millions C$)

Flows (a)	Details	(1)	(2)
(1)	Sales to the United States by U.S. Subsidiaries in Canada (Table A4.2)	23,270	
(2)	Other Foreign Sales by U.S. Subsidiaries in Canada (Table A4.2)	4,968	
	Sub-Total (Table A4.2)	28,238	28,238
(3)	Purchases from Parent Groups in Canada by Canada's Affiliates in the United States (Table A4.2)		6,405
	Sub-Total (Table A4.3)		34,643
	Less:		
(4)	Purchases from the United States by U.S. Subsidiaries in Canada (Table A4.4)	26,913	
(5)	Other Foreign Purchases by U.S. Subsidiaries in Canada (Table A4.4)	5,538	
	Sub-Total (Table A4.5)	32,451	32,451
	Benefits of Canada's Balance of Trade (Table A4.5)		2,192
(6)	Purchases by Canada's Parents from their Affiliates in the United States (Table A4.6)		1,164
	Net Benefit of the Balance of Trade (Table A4.6)		1,029

Source: See Notes Table 4.1

Table A4.2
Foreign Sales by U.S. Subsidiaries in Canada
(millions C$)

Year	(1) Sales to the United States by U.S. Canada (a)	(2) Other Foreign Sales by U. S. Subsidiaries in Canada	(3) Total Foreign Sales
1984	23,270 (b)	4,968	28,238 (c)
1983	20,892 (b)	4,406	25,298 (c)
1982	18,758 (b)	3,906	22,664 (c)
1981	16,841	3,464	20,305
1980	15,682	3,735	19,417
1979	15,845	2,999	18,844
1978	15,658	2,355	18,013
1977	13,222	2,039	15,261
1976	11,413	1,760	13,173
1975	9,448	2,011	11,459

Notes: (a) Market Rate/Par or Central Rate exchange rates used; International Monetary Fund, *International Financial Statistics: Yearbook* (1986): 257.

(b) Data for 1982, 1983 and 1984 extrapolated based on the averages for 5 years (8.37%) and 14 years (14.39%) of 11.38%.

(c) Data for 1982, 1983 and 1984 extrapolated based on the average for five years (9.22%) and 17 years (14.01%) of 11.62%.

Sources: See Table 4.1 in main text.

Canada of this bilateral trade, including intra-industry trade (flows 1, 3, 4, and 6), has been Cdn. $1,740 million. A brief discussion of table A4.2 to A4.6 follows. The data in the tables can be matched up to the flows in the "Details" column in table A4.1 where the data sources are indicated in brackets.

Table A4.2 presents data on U.S. subsidiaries sales to the United States (column 1) and to other countries (column 2). Since 1975, the total foreign sales of U.S. subsidiaries in Canada has increased from Cdn. $11,459 million to Cdn. $28,238 million in 1984. Table A4.3 adds total foreign sales by these U.S. corporations (column 1) to the purchases by the Canadian affiliates in the United States from their parent groups (sales by parents to affiliates) in column 2. This gives Canada's "Balance on Foreign Sales" (column

Table A4.3
The Balance of Foreign Sales for Canada by U.S. Subsidiaries in Canada and
Canada's Affiliates in the United States (millions C$)

Year	(1) Foreign Sales by U.S. Subsidiaries in Canada (a)	(2) Purchases from Parent Groups in Canada by Canada's Affiliates in the United States	(3) Canada's Balance on Foreign Sales
1984	28,238 (b)	6,405	34,643
1983	25,298 (b)	5,422	30,720
1982	22,664 (b)	5,186	27,850
1981	20,305	6,477	26,782
1980	19,417	5,447	24,864
1979	18,844	5,101	23,945
1978	18,013	4,629	22,642
1977	15,261	3,612	18,873
1976	13,173	3,190 (c)	16,363
1975	11,459	3,078 (c)	14,537

Notes: (a) From column (3) of Table A4.2.

(b) Data for 1982, 1983, and 1984 extrapolated based on the averages for five years (9.22%) and 17 years (14.01%) of 11.62%.

(c) Data for 1976 and 1975 extrapolated backwards based on averages of the growth from 1977 to 1980 (2.74%) and from 1981 to 1984 (11.51%) of 4.39%.

Sources: See Table 4.1 main text.

3), which has grown from Cdn. $14,537 million in 1975, to Cdn. $34,643 million in 1984.

Table A4.4 presents data on the purchases of U.S. subsidiaries from the United States (column 1) and from other countries (column 2). Since 1975, the total foreign purchases of U.S. subsidiaries in Canada has increased from Cdn. $11,736 million to Cdn. $32,451 million in 1984.

Table A4.5 reports the "Benefits of Canada's Balance of Trade." This is derived by deducting the foreign purchases of the U.S. subsidiaries in Canada (derived in table A4.4) from "Canada's Balance on Foreign Sales" (column 3 of table A4.3). Since 1982, this balance of trade has been, on average, Cdn. $2,250 million.

In order to arrive at the net benefit of Canada's balance of trade of its affiliates in the United States and the U.S. sub-

Table A4.4
Foreign Purchases by U.S. Subsidiaries in Canada (millions C$)

Year	(1) Purchases from the United States by U.S. Subsidiaries In Canada	(2) Other Foreign Purchases by the U.S. Subsidiaries in Canada	(3) Total Foreign Purchases
1984	26,913 (a)	5,538	32,451 (b)
1983	24,137 (a)	4,538	28,675 (b)
1982	21,648 (a)	3,690	25,338 (b)
1981	19,415	2,974	22,389
1980	17,917	2,276	20,193
1979	19,138	1,486	20,624
1978	16,783	1,293	18,076
1977	14,295	1,319	15,614
1976	12,513	1,302	13,815
1975	10,492	1,244	11,736

Notes: (a) Data for 1982, 1983 and 1984 extrapolated based on the average
for 5 years (9.02%) and 14 years (13.97%) of 11.50%.

(b) Data for 1982, 1983 and 1984 extrapolated based on the average
for 5 years (10.34%) and 14 years (16.00%) of 13.17%.

Sources: See Table 4.1 main text.

sidiaries in Canada, it is still necessary to deduct the purchases by the Canadian parent groups from their affiliates
in the United States. This is done in table A4.6. From 1982
to 1984 these purchases have averaged Cdn. $1,028 million.
As already indicated, table A4.6 demonstrates that Canada
receives a benefit from U.S. subsidiaries operating in Canada and Canadian companies operating their own affiliates
in the United States. Thus table A4.6 confirms the results of
table 4.1. There is a substantial net benefit to Canada from
its involvement in international trade and investment.

METHODOLOGICAL NOTES TO THE APPENDIX

The data in tables A4.2 to A4.6 consist of the actual data
gathered from the sources listed at the end of the Appendix
plus estimated amounts for the years that were missing
from the data sets. From the DRIE data, the years 1982 to
1984 are not available. Therefore, in order to extrapolate for
these years we find the mean of the average growth rates for

Table A4.5

The Benefits of the Balance of Trade on Foreign Sales by Canada
and Purchases by U.S. Subsidiaries in Canada (millions C$)

Year	(1) Canada's Balance on Foreign Sales (a)	(2) Foreign Purchases by U.S. Subsidiaries in Canada (b)	(3) Benefits of Canada's Balance of Trade
1984	34,643	32,451 (c)	2,192
1983	30,720	28,675 (c)	2,045
1982	27,850	25,338 (c)	2,512
1981	26,782	22,389	4,393
1980	24,864	20,193	4,671
1979	23,945	20,624	3,321
1978	22,642	18,076	4,566
1977	18,873	15,614	3,259
1976	16,363	13,815	2,548
1975	14,537	11,736	2,801

Notes: (a) From column (3) of Table A4.3.

(b) From column (3) of Table A4.4.

(c) Data for 1982, 1983 and 1984 extrapolated based on the average
for 5 years (10.34%) and 14 years (16.00%) of 13.17%.

Sources: See Table 4.1 in main text.

five years and the largest period available for this data set,
which ranges from 14 to 17 years.

For example, the data for the years 1982 to 1984, in column 1 of table A4.2, were derived from the mean of the average growth rates for fives years (8.37 percent) and for 14
years (14.39 percent), which equals 11.38 percent. By multi-
plying the 1981 sales figure (Cdn. $16,841 million) by 11.38
percent, we obtain the sales figures for 1982 of Cdn. $18,758
million. This figure is then multiplied by 11.38 percent to
obtain sales of Cdn. $20,892 million for 1983 and so on.
Similarly the Department of Commerce data in column 2 of
table A4.3 is extrapolated backwards in order to obtain 1976
and 1975 data, except the rate is based on the mean of the
average growth rates from 1977 to 1980 and from 1981 to
1984.

Table A4.6

The Net Benefit on the Balance of Trade for Canada by U.S. Subsidiaries and
Canadian Affiliates (millions C$)

Year	(1) Benefits of Canada's Balance of Trade (a)	(2) Purchases by the Canadian Parents from their Affiliates in the United States (Costs) (b)	(3) Net Benefit of Canada's Balance of Trade
1984	2,192	1,164	1,028
1983	2,045	1,009	1,036
1982	2,512	910	1,602
1981	4,393	1,101	3,292
1980	4,671	1,139	3,532
1979	3,321	1,126	2,195
1978	4,566	848	3,718
1977	3,259	497	2,762
1976	2,548	400 (c)	2,148
1975	2,801	352 (c)	2,449

Notes: (a) From column (3) of Table A4.5.

(b) Market Rate/Par or Central Rate exchange rates used; International Monetary Fund, *International Financial Statistics: Yearbook* (1986): 257.

(c) Data for 1976 and 1975 extrapolated backwards based on averages of the growth from 1977 to 1980 (31.15%) and from 1981 to 1984 2.04% of 14.55%.

Sources: See Table 4.1 in main text.

The **DRIE** data cover the largest 300 foreign-owned enterprises (900 to 1,000 individual firms) in Canada. In order to check its validity the DRIE data were compared with U.S. Department of Commerce data collected on U.S. subsidiaries and published for various years in *U.S. Direct Investment Abroad.* This publication first appeared in 1977 and again in 1982 as a benchmark survey. Since 1982 it has appeared bi-annually as, *U.S. Direct Investment Abroad: Operations of U.S. Parent Companies and Their Foreign Affiliates, Preliminary* and *Revised Estimates.* The *Preliminary 1984 Estimates,* published in October 1986, is the latest edition available.

The Department of Commerce data suggests that the DRIE data are understated by 15 to 30 percent. For example, in 1977 (the only year for which the DRIE and Department of Commerce data are available for comparison) DRIE reported the foreign sales by U.S. subsidiaries in Canada as Cdn. $15,261 million (column 3, table A4.2), whereas the Department of Commerce reported the foreign sales as U.S. $18,258 million (Cdn. $19,981 million) Adjusting for the Commerce data would increase "Canada's Balance on Foreign Sales" in Column three of table A4.3 from Cdn. $18,873 million to Cdn. $23,593 million.

Similarly, the Department of Commerce reported the foreign purchases by the U.S. subsidiaries in Canada as U.S. $18,215 million (Cdn. $19,934 million) versus the Cdn. $15,614 million reported by DRIE (column 3, table A4.4). Adjusting for this would increase the "Benefits of Canada's Balance of Trade" (column 3 of table A4.5) from Cdn. $3,259 million to Cdn. $3,659 million. When this figure is transferred into Column 1 of table A4.6, it increases the "Net Benefit of Canada's Balance of Trade" in column 3 by Cdn. $400 million, from Cdn. $2,762 million to Cdn. $3,162 million.

Chapter 5

The Billion Dollar Club:
Large Foreign-Owned Subsidiaries in Canada and the United States

A major premise of this study is that many of the adjustment costs of bilateral trade liberalization are borne by a group of the very largest multinational enterprises. Who are these firms and how will they respond to a new trading regime? Identified in this chapter are all the U.S.-owned subsidiaries in Canada with sales in excess of Cdn. $1 billion and all the Canadian-owned multinationals with sales of over Cdn. $1 billion. As we shall see, using 1986 data, the billion dollar club consists of 14 U.S.-owned subsidiaries in Canada plus 22 Canadian-owned multinationals operating in the United States. The size, foreign sales, exports, financial performance, and the relevant attributes of these corporations are discussed in this chapter. For a more in-depth examination of some of these firms and their corporate strategies, see Rugman and McIlveen (1985) and Rugman and Warner (1988). This chapter and chapter 6 are intended to give a more general description of the financial and export performance of these firms. The results of a questionnaire sent to all these 36 companies are reported and discussed in chapter 6.

IDENTIFICATION AND PERFORMANCE OF
FOREIGN-OWNED SUBSIDIARIES IN CANADA
In order to gain a richer appreciation of the actual multinational enterprises involved in the adjustment process, this section identifies and analyzes the performance of the largest U.S.-owned subsidiaries in Canada. The "sample" of foreign-owned firms studied is the entire set of U.S. industrial subsidiaries with sales in excess of Cdn. $1 billion for 1986, the latest year for which firm-level information is available (from the 1987 Annual Reports of these companies). This information is arranged conveniently in several annual directories, such as the *Financial Post 500*, which

is compiled entirely from information revealed in company annual reports.

This information is reliable since publicly held companies must report accounting information according to recognized standards. According to basic tenents of finance theory these publicly available data are subsequently reflected in the stock market prices of the shares of these companies. It is also recognized by financial analysts that the use of such accounting data over a long time period, for example five or ten years, will permit a reasonable market-based analysis of financial performance. Given the efficiency of the stock market, in its ability to incorporate all publicly available information into the stock prices of the company, it is impossible over time for the management of a company to persistently disguise the costs, revenues, and profits of the firm. Therefore, the performance of a company, subsidiary as well as parent, can be assessed using conventional financial measures. Data such as the return on equity (ROE) for the 1982–1986 and 1977–1986 periods will be reported here, in order to help judge the ability of subsidiaries (and their parents) to adjust to a new trading environment. In addition, some basic data on the research and development (R & D) performance of the U.S. subsidiaries and their parents is also reported, again for several years, to develop an understanding of the technological capabilities and potential responsiveness of these firms to trade liberalization.

These factors provide clues to the ability of the strategic planners of the corporations to respond efficiently to changes in the trading system. The missing dimension from this analysis is the attitude of the senior managers in the subsidiaries and also in the parent firms. There is some evidence that the strategic planners of U.S.-owned subsidiaries operate with relatively little autonomy (D'Cruz 1986). If this is the case then an understanding of the sales, performance, and management style of the U.S. parent firms will be necessary in order to form judgments about responsiveness to bilateral trade liberalization. While these issues are examined in detail in chapter 6, here basic data on the parent multinationals are reported to lay the factual groundwork for such future analysis.

Table 5.1 lists the set of U.S. industrial subsidiaries in Canada with sales of over Cdn. $1 billion in 1986. Retail service firms such as Sears, Woolworth, K-Mart, A and P, and Safeway, all of which had sales over Cdn. $1 billion, are excluded. Also excluded is the telephone utility, Anglo-Canadian Tel. Given the nature of their business the strategic responses to free trade will be mainly neutral compared to the industrial corporations. By limiting the survey to the industrial subsidiaries the list of U.S. subsidiaries examined rests at 14.

Also reported in table 5.1 are the sales of the parent firms, and the ratio of subsidiary to parent sales, which averages nearly 10 percent. The largest U.S. subsidiary, General Motors of Canada, has sales of nearly Cdn. $18.5 billion and ranks at number 31 in the *Fortune* "International 500" list for 1986. Other subsidiaries in the *Fortune* top 100, are Ford of Canada (43rd), and Chrysler Canada (96th). In all there are 19 U.S. subsidiaries with sales over Cdn. $1 billion listed on the *Fortune 500*, in 1986. Of these 8 are in manufacturing categories (including 3 in automobiles), 6 in energy, 4 in retailing, and 1 in restaurant hospitality. The concern of this study, however, will be only with the 14 industrial U.S. subsidiaries.

The percentage of foreign ownership of these 14 subsidiaries is reported in the *Financial Post 500*. All are more than 50 percent foreign-owned. It is 100 percent for 7 firms: General Motors, Chrysler, IBM, Amoco, Mobil, Dow Chemical, and Procter and Gamble. The remaining firms also have high degrees of ownership by their parent firms, including 70 percent by Exxon, 92 percent by G.E., 73 percent by Du Pont, 91 percent by Cargill, and 94 percent by Ford.

Table 5.2 provided some evidence that the U.S. subsidiaries in Canada are not purely branch plants selling entirely to the Canadian markets. On average this set of the largest subsidiaries export over 36 percent of their output. While the retailers do not provide information on their exports it is reasonable to assume that they do not export very much. However, such distributors would not be expected to export and most of the criticism of branch plants and deindustrialization has been directed towards the foreign-owned industrial firms. Yet, their export perfor-

Table 5.1

The Largest Canadian Subsidiaries of U.S. Multinationals

Subsidiary (% Foreign Ownership)	Parent	1986 Sales (millions of Cdn $) Subsidiary	1986 Sales (millions of Cdn $) Parent	Subsidiary's sales as % of Parent's	Rank based on % sales
General Motors of Canada (100)	GM	18,533	142,397	13.02	3
Ford Motor Co. of Canada (94)	Ford	14,327	86,861	16.49	2
Chrysler Canada (100)	Chrysler	7,359	31,181	23.60	1
Imperial Oil (70)	Exxon	6,964	96,795	7.19	6
IBM Canada (100)	IBM	2,924	70,981	4.12	10
Texaco Canada (79)	Texaco	2,719	43,784	6.21	7
Mobil Oil Canada (100)	Mobil Oil	1,648	62,139	2.65	13
Canadian General Electric (92)	G.E.	1,642	48,767	3.37	11
Dow Chemical Canada (100)	Dow	1,352	15,392	8.78	5
Amoco Canada (100)	Amoco	1,325	25,319	5.23	8
Du Pont (73)	Du Pont	1,243	37,600	3.31	12
Cargill (91)	Cargill	1,201	N/A	N/A	N/A
Suncor (75)	Sun Co.	1,150	12,986	8.86	4
Procter & Gamble (100)	Procter & Gamble	1,060	21,383	4.96	9
Total		74,129	814,401	Mean = 9.2	

Sources: Subsidiaries' sales are from the "Financial Post" 500, April 27, 1987. Parent sales are from the "Fortune" 500 (April 27, 1987 and June 8, 1987). U.S. dollars have been translated to Cdn. dollars using the IMF's "International Financial Statistics Yearbook (1987)" year end exchange rate, 1.3805

Table 5.2

Export Sales Performance of the Largest Canadian
Subsidiaries of U.S. Multinationals

Canadian Subsidiary	Average Ratio of Exports to Total Sales, 1984–1986 (%)	
	Subsidiary	Parent
G.M. Canada	63.0	17.8 a
Ford of Canada	51.5	35.5 a
Chrysler Canada	63.8	0.5
Imperial Oil	0	56.1 a
IBM Canada	28.5**	44.7 a
Texaco Canada	0	48.8 a
Mobil Oil Canada	24.3***	61.2 a
C.G.E.	11.5	10.9
Dow Chemical	0	51.9 a
Amoco	private	21.4 a
Du Pont Canada	14.8	9.4
Cargill	N/A	N/A
Suncor	30.0*	20.5 a
Procter & Gamble	0	26.0 a
	0	
Mean	35.9	31.9

Notes: All figures for parent companies are foreign sales to total sales ratio.
       * 1986 figure only
      ** 1985, 1986 figures only
     *** 1983, 1984, 1986 figures only
      a: foreign to total sales (no export statistics available)

Sources: Corporate Annual Reports unless otherwise noted.

mance is exemplary. Indeed, these U.S. manufacturing subsidiaries export more than Canadian-owned firms (since the
ratio of export to GNP in Canada is also about 30 percent).
Canada's 22 largest multinationals actually export 39 percent on average (see table 5.6).

The nine subsidiaries for which export data are available also export more, on average, than their parent firms.
The three parent firms with export data have average exports of only 7 percent of sales. However, the set of parent
multinationals have an average ratio of foreign to total sales
of 32 percent, where foreign sales include both exports by
the parent firm plus sales of its overseas subsidiaries.

In general, these data indicate that the typical large U.S. subsidiary in Canada contributes to Canada's trade in a similar manner as a large domestic firm. (Data on individual imports are not available but DRIE data on aggressive imports, reported elsewhere, suggest that imports probably match exports.) The data certainly do not support the notion that these large subsidiaries are purely branch plants located in Canada to service the Canadian market alone. Indeed, the subsidiaries are internationally active and their response to trade liberalization will be largely conditioned by their trade performance.

Table 5.3 examines the financial performance of the largest U.S. subsidiaries in Canada during the periods 1982–1986 and 1977–1986. The measure of performance used is the return on equity (ROE). Return is defined as the net income after taxes and equity as the year-end book value of shareholder's equity. Two financial indicators of mean earnings and variability of earnings are generated from these data. First, as a measure of return the mean value of the 5 and 10 year ROE is used. Second, as a proxy for total risk the standard deviation (SD) about the mean for the 5 and 10 year ROE is used. These two financial indicators are reported for each of the subsidiaries.

In table 5.3, the average ROE for these firms is reported as 15.3 percent, and the average SD is 6.3 percent.[1] In contrast, the average ROE for the parent firms is similar at 14.7 percent and the SD for U.S. parent firms is 4.0 percent. The averages exclude Chrysler Corporation due to its extraordinarily high SDs which distort the averages. These results confirm earlier work by Rugman (1980b, 1981, 1985b, 1986) and others, which reports that the profits of parent multinational enterprises average around 12–15 percent and that there is no significant difference between the ROE of multinationals and of domestic firms, of similar size, in the United States and Canada. Further, this earlier work also

---

1. In order to calculate the standard deviation (SD) for the return on equity (ROE) of the U.S. subsidiaries and the Canadian multinationals in Tables 5.3 and 5.7, respectively, the formula used is: $SD = \sqrt{(x - \bar{x})^2/n - 1}$ where $\bar{x}$ is the mean for $n = 10$ years. All negative ROEs have been set to zero, but are still included in the calculation of the SD in order to reflect the full ten years and is the R & D for the given year of observations.

Table 5.3

Financial Performance of the Largest Canadian Subsidiaries of U.S. Multinationals 1982-1987

Subsidiary	1982-1986				1977-1986			
	Subsidiary ROE		Parent ROE		Subsidiary ROE		Parent ROE	
	Mean	S.D.	Mean	S.D.	Mean	S.D.	Mean	S.D.
G.M. of Canada	33.5	22.2	13.8	5.6	26.5	19.7	12.7	7.6
Ford of Canada	16.1	11.2	21.6	11.4	9.0	10.7	15.5	11.6
Chrysler Canada	130.9	193.4	60.5	46.8	65.8	51.5	30.8	44.5
Imperial Oil	9.5	2.7	17.0	1.4	13.2	4.9	17.2	2.8
IBM Canada (1)	28.8	11.9	22.4	4.2	25.5	8.7	21.6	3.3
Texaco Canada	17.4	3.4	6.9	2.7	19.3	8.2	10.8	5.4
Mobil Oil Canada	16.7	4.7	9.2	1.0	20.6	6.6	13.2	5.2
Canadian General Electric	9.5	1.3	18.3	0.8	10.3	1.4	18.4	0.6
Dow Chemical Canada (2)	2.1	2.1	8.4	4.6	10.0	10.5	4.2	4.6
Amoco Canada	18.7	2.0	19.1	8.0	18.9	3.8	18.2	5.9
Du Pont Canada	10.8	6.6	10.3	1.5	12.8	8.5	12.4	2.8
Suncor	5.9	3.8	11.0	3.7	11.2	9.3	13.7	4.5
Procter & Gamble	15.1	3.4	18.2	2.9	17.9	4.2	16.0	2.3
Mean	15.3	6.3	14.7	4.0	14.5	8.0	14.5	4.7

Notes: Negative ROE figures have been set to zero.

Chrysler has been excluded from the means of all companies.

(1) 4 year and 9 year averages respectively

(2) 3 year and 8 year averages respectively

Sources: Data for subsidiaries is from "The Financial Post 500," 1983-various issues.

Data for the parent companies is from "The Fortune 500," various issues and Corporate Annual Reports.

detected greater risk in the earnings of U.S. subsidiaries in Canada. This reflects the greater perception of risk in the relatively thinner Canadian stock market and smaller economic system when compared to the large and more diversified U.S. stock market and economy. Indeed, previous research (Rugman 1979) indicated that the relatively smaller size of the Canadian economy led to higher risk being experienced by both domestic and foreign-owned firms in Canada. The difference in variability of earnings also reflects the greater opportunities for international diversification by U.S. multinationals, which are active in more foreign markets than their Canadian subsidiaries (who mainly sell to the United States, whose economy is highly correlated with Canada's).

The conclusion to be drawn from the data in table 5.3 is that U.S.-owned subsidiaries in Canada are efficient. They are not earning excess profits vis-à-vis their parents, neither are they being squeezed by their parents to bolster home country profits of the U.S. parent. The latter point is indirect evidence that transfer pricing and other devices to manipulate parent-subsidiary profits are not being used by U.S. multinationals. Further evidence supporting the lack of transfer pricing in this period for U.S. oil firms in Canada, appears in Rugman and Eden (1985).

A final issue worthy of attention is the alleged lack of R & D by U.S. subsidiaries in Canada. In table 5.4 data are reported for the ratio of R & D to sales for these U.S. subsidiaries in Canada for 1985. These data are difficult to acquire. For the nine subsidiaries for which it is available the ratio is 1.27 percent, while for 13 parent firms it is significantly higher at 3.24 percent.

These results are similar to an earlier study (Rugman 1981), where the mean R & D to sales percentages for 12 subsidiaries was 1.19 percent and for their parents, 3.12 percent. However, in that study it was found that the R & D ratio for a group of similarly sized Canadian-owned multinationals was only 2.07 percent. Similarly the mean R & D to sales ratio for Canada's 20 megafirms was 1.4 percent (Rugman and McIlveen 1985, table 2.2).

This evidence on R & D is not central to the theme of this study, which examines trade-related aspects of adjust-

Table 5.4

R & D Performance of the Largest Canadian Subsidiaries
of U.S. Multinationals, 1985

Canadian Subsidiary	R & D as % of Sales	
	Subsidiary	Parent
G.M. Canada	0.15	3.47 (a)
Ford Canada	N/A	3.82 (b)
Imperial Oil	0.89	0.74 (b)
Chrysler Canada	N/A	2.86 (b)
Texaco Canada	3.07 (b)	2.33 (a)
IBM Canada	2.83	6.91 (b)
Amoco Canada	N/A	0.73 (b)
Mobil Oil Canada	N/A	0.30 (a)
Cargill	0.03 (b)	N/A
Canadian General Electric	1.31	9.00 (b)
Suncor	0.85	0.30
Dow Chemical Canada	1.23	4.80 (b)
Du Pont Canada	1.09	3.88 (b)
Procter & Gamble	N/A	2.96 (b)
Mean =	1.27	3.24

Notes: (a) 1979–1981 average, otherwise just for 1985

(b) Derived from Annual Reports.

Sources: "Canada's Leading R & D Spenders," *The Financial Post* (Section 4, October 25, 1986): p. 37.

Annual Reports

ment. However, it is important to keep in perspective the basic reasons for multinational activity, both in Canada and the United States. Foreign direct investment is an alternative means to exporting in order to secure access to a market. Both methods allow the parent firm to control the rate of use of its firm-specific advantage, which is usually knowledge based in either production or marketing skills. A complete lack of R & D in the subsidiaries would be an indication of a lack of ability to adapt and commercialize existing technologies to new product lines. However, this is not the case. The U.S. subsidiaries in Canada do nearly as much R & D as Canadian-owned firms. They are therefore well placed to adapt to changes in the trade environment.

The ability of the U.S.-owned subsidiaries to adapt to trade liberalization is further strengthened by the knowledge that they have been increasing their ability to secure world product mandates. Previous work has criticized the advocates of world product mandating for overstating their case and ignoring the managerial difficulties involved in rearranging the organizational structures of multinationals to accommodate such decentralized R & D (Rugman 1983a; Poynter and Rugman 1982; and Rugman and Douglas 1986). However, it is apparent that most U.S. subsidiaries in Canada are successful exporters and should no longer be viewed as purely branch plants. Although managerial autonomy may still be low (D'Cruz 1983) it is reasonable to believe that bilateral trade liberalization could result in an increased amount of intra-firm trade. This would facilitate the possible acceleration of reorganization of internal structures to place more responsibility for the development, production, and marketing of new product lines (i.e., a world product mandate) in subsidiaries. This trend to decentralization in R & D, coupled with increased managerial autonomy for strategic planning in the subsidiaries, is already underway (D'Cruz 1986) and it should be speeded up by trade liberalization.

CANADIAN-OWNED MULTINATIONALS IN THE UNITED STATES

The burden of adjustment after trade liberalization, will be borne by Canadian-owned multinational enterprises as well as the subsidiaries of U.S.-owned corporations in Canada. In this section attention is focused upon the identity, nature, performance, and trade-related characteristics of the largest Canadian-owned multinationals, all of which have extensive operations in the United States. Firm-level data, from published sources based on information from company annual reports, will be used to accomplish the following.

First, the largest 22 Canadian-owned multinational enterprises (all those with annual sales of over Cdn. $1 billion) will be identified. Next the nature of their international operations and extent of their multinationality, including exporting and subsidiary production will be discussed.

Also reviewed will be their financial performance, number of employees, and related aspects of efficiency. This information is necessary to assess the manner in which these specific corporations would adjust to new trading regimes.

This section builds on the more aggregate data used in the second half of chapter 3. Those data were drawn from the U.S. Department of Commerce annual survey of all foreign-owned affiliates in the United States. Included in the Commerce data is the entire set of Canadian multinationals (i.e., a broader group than the 22 firms specifically identified in this section). There are over 1,000 individual affiliates of Canadian-owned companies currently operating in the United States, although the number of parent firms is much less than this.

The major objective of this study is to investigate the precise nature of intra-firm trade, namely the sales between Canadian parent firms and their U.S. subsidiaries. Study of these specific large multinationals throws light on the earlier work on the index of intra-industry production and the new bilateral index of national balance of production (calculated in chapter 4). The extent to which the great degree of interdependence between the U.S. and Canadian economies may serve to reduce any adjustment costs associated with trade liberalization is discussed with reference to these leading firms.

Identification of the Canadian Multinationals

Table 5.5 lists the set of the largest 22 Canadian-owned multinational enterprises. The largest Canadian industrial multinationals are identified from the *Fortune* "International 500" list of non-U.S. industrial corporations. This list is more reliable than similar Canadian sources, since the latter excludes categories such as utilities and retailing operations. The *Fortune* listing was then verified against the *Financial Post* "Industry's 500" listing. Excluded from analysis is the Canadian financial and banking sector, although the methodology used here could be applied to these international companies at a future date.

The list is restricted to the largest Canadian-owned "industrial" multinationals in 1986. The 1987 *Fortune* list of the largest foreign industrial corporations in 1986, contains

Table 5.5

Identification of Largest Canadian-Owned Multinationals

Firm	1986 Sales or Revenue (Millions of CDN. $)
Alcan	8222
Northern Telecom	6091
Seagram	4618
John Labatt	4253
Gulf Canada	3980
Noranda	3547
Moore	2919
Abitibi-Price	2764
Nova	2681
MacMillan Bloedel	2512
Domtar	2327
Molson	2250
Consolidated-Bathurst	2018
Ivaco	1945
Varity	1877
AMCA International	1498
Inco	1452
Cominco	1328
Falconbridge	1146
Bombardier	1104
Canfor	1047
Magna International	1028
Total	60607

Notes: The methodology underlying the selection of these firms is explained in Chapter 2 of Rugman and McIlveen, 1985.

Some figures have been restated from U.S. dollars to Canadian dollars using year-end exchange rates. In 1986, Gulf Canada held an 83 percent interest in Abitibi-Price. The total sales for Abitibi are included by Gulf in its own sales and hence the overall total includes some double-counting.

Sources: Data from Corporate Annual Reports, and the *Financial Post 500*. The exchange rate is from the *IMF Financial Statistics Yearbook, 1986*.

31 corporations designated as Canadian-owned. From 1980 to 1987 the Canadian industrial corporations have been able to maintain their numerical position on the *Fortune* list relative to the other four major industrial countries.

These include Japan with 152 corporations, the United Kingdom with 72 corporations, and West Germany and France with 53 and 41 corporations respectively. Between 1980 and 1986, of the 10 major contributors to the *Fortune* list, only Japan has been able to increase its share relative to the other countries (by 31 corporations). The major declines were from the U.K., West Germany, and France, which between them lost 26 corporations, including 11 in the top 100, and Sweden, which lost 4 of its 26 corporations, over the same period. Over this period Canada has lost only one overall and none from the top 100.

The group of 31 Canadian multinationals in the *Fortune* list is reduced to 23 when the Canadian subsidiaries of foreign-controlled companies are excluded. Foreign ownership is defined as being greater than 50 percent, unless the corporation is widely held. Under this criterion, both Ivaco and Alcan, with 65 and 54 percent foreign ownership respectively, and Varity with 85 percent foreign ownership, remain on the list of Canadian industrial corporations. However, three foreign-owned automotive manufacturers are eliminated: General Motors of Canada, Ford of Canada, and Chrysler Canada. Also eliminated are three petroleum firms: Imperial Oil, Texaco Canada, and Mobil Oil. Finally, two electronics manufacturers, Canadian General Electric and IBM, Canada are eliminated.

Not all of the 23 remaining firms are multinationals. In order to determine whether they are a multinational firm, two criteria are applied. First, the firm must have production facilities in at least one foreign country. Second, the firm must derive a minimum of 25 percent of its total sales from foreign markets. These foreign sales are defined as exports plus sales made by foreign subsidiaries. It would be preferable to isolate sales made by the foreign subsidiary(s), but most company annual reports present insufficient segmented accounting information to distinguish between exports and foreign subsidiary sales.

Under these criteria for multinationality, seven additional firms from the original 1986 *Fortune* list have been removed. These are: Petro-Canada and the Canada Development Corporation—two crown corporations; Stelco and Dofasco—two steel corporations; Canada Packers—food

products; Dome Petroleum—petroleum (which is also removed due to its 60 percent foreign ownership); and International Thomson—publishing.

An exception to the multinational criteria was made for
John Labatt, which only had an average foreign to total
sales ratio (F/T) of 19.6 percent for the four years of data
available. However, for the last two years Labatt's F/T ratio
rose to 25.3 percent for 1985 and 31.8 percent for 1986.
None of the other firms satisfied the benchmarks for multinationality, although all of them had some degree of foreign
activity. The Canadian industrial multinationals list, therefore, stands at 16 from the original *Fortune* source.

The list was expanded to 22 on the basis of two further
important criteria. First, two multinationals were deleted
because of their status as conglomerates—Canadian Pacific
and IMASCO. IMASCO as a conglomerate, also has an F/T
ratio of less than 25 percent. Canadian Pacific's large size
(Cdn. $11.0 billion in sales for 1985) and wide corporate di-
versification prevent meaningful analysis from being done.
Instead, the two largest multinational subsidiaries of Canadian Pacific (AMCA International and Cominco) are included as separate firms.

Second, further additions to the list were also required
after consulting the *Financial Post's* "Industry 500" survey,
since Nova Corporation (1986 sales of Cdn. $2.7 billion),
which would have placed it in the 155th position on the *Fortune* "International 500" list was not included. While Nova's
F/T ratio from 1982 to 1986 was only 19.1 percent, from
1980 to 1986 its average F/T ratio was 27.8 percent; therefore, we waived the F/T criteria. Another company, Abitibi-
Price, would have ranked 154th, with sales just over Cdn.
$2.7 billion. Also omitted from the *Fortune* listing were Ma-
gna International, Bombardier, Falconbridge, and Canfor; all
of which had sales exceeding Cdn. $1 billion as reported in
table 5.5. The final list of the largest Canadian-owned "industrial" multinational firms stands at 22 firms, as listed in
table 5.5.

Of the original list of 96 firms with sales greater than
Cdn. $1 billion, as indicated in the *Financial Post* "Industry
500" survey, the largest 22 "industrial" Canadian-owned
multinational corporations account for 21 percent of the

sales of Canadian registered corporations with sales greater than Cdn. $1 billion in 1986.

Degree of Multinationality of Canada's Multinationals

The Canadian industrial multinationals are active in foreign markets through both exporting from Canada and production abroad. These key types of international activity, representing the degree of multinationality, are reported in table 5.6. There are two measures of multinationality: foreign subsidiary sales (S) to total sales (T); and, exports (X) to total sales (T). When added together, the (S/T) plus (X/T) ratios give the foreign to total sales (F/T) ratio. While it would be preferable to utilize only the subsidiary to total sales ratios, due to the lack of published disaggregated data on foreign subsidiary production, it is necessary to utilize the (F/T) ratio.

The average F/T ratio for the 20 corporations for which data were available is 67 percent. Nine of the firms have an F/T ratio greater than 75 percent. Eight companies have an F/T ratio falling between 50 and 75 percent. Three have an F/T ratio between 25 and 50 percent and two have an F/T ratio under 25 percent.

The average S/T ratio for the 12 multinationals that reported this data is 29 percent. For two corporations the S/T ratio is greater than 55 percent: AMCA International (78) and Ivaco (60).

Performance of the Canadian Multinationals

Table 5.7 reports data on the sales, number of employees and return on equity (ROE) for the 22 Canadian multinationals. Three corporations have had a continuous positive growth rate in sales over this period. These include: Alcan, Northern Telecom, and Gulf. Many of the corporations experienced a decline in their sales in the 1980 to 1982 period, particularly in 1982. Three companies have been facing declining sales in the last several years, Cominco from Cdn. $1.6 billion in 1984 to Cdn. $1.3 billion in 1986, Nova, from Cdn. $3.8 billion in 1983 to Cdn. $2.7 billion in 1986 and AMCA International from Cdn. $1.6 billion in 1985 to $1.0 billion in 1986. However, these

Table 5.6

Degree of Multinationality of the Largest Canadian Industrial Multinationals, 1982–1986

Firm	(S/T) Average Ratio of Foreign Subsidiary Sales to Total Sales (1) (%)	(X/T) Average Ratio of Exports to Total Sales (1) (%)	(F/T) Average Ratio of Foreign to Total Sales (%)
Alcan	n/a	n/a	82.0
Northern Telecom	n/a	n/a	65.3
Seagram	n/a	n/a	94.0
John Labatt (3)	n/a	n/a	19.6
Gulf Canada (2)	7.5	19.5	27.0
Noranda	39.9	25.3	65.1
Moore	n/a	n/a	90.2
Abitibi-Price	19.3	44.5	63.8
Nova	n/a	n/a	19.1
MacMillan Bloedel	27.8	52.8	80.6
Domtar	12.7	18.5	31.2
Molson	n/a	n/a	28.8
Consolidated-Bathurst	23.7	56.6	80.4
Ivaco	59.3	19.9	79.1
Varity	n/a	n/a	92.7
AMCA International	61.1	2.0	63.0
Inco	n/a	N/a	83.6
Cominco	29.0	45.4	74.4
Falconbridge	n/a	n/a	72.7
Bombardier	17.2	56.3	73.5
Canfor	17.9	46.9	64.8
Magna International	20.2	65.4	78.5
Average	29.3	39.4	66.7

Notes: (1) S/T and X/T data are not generally available as F/T data in firm's annual report.
(2) Gulf excluded because of change of ownership in 1985. 3 year data used for Gulf.
(3) 4 year data used for Labatt.

Source: Corporate Annual Reports.

Table 5.7
Performance of the Largest Canadian Industrial Multinationals

Firm	Average Sales 1981–1986 (millions of Cdn $)	Number of Employees		Profits (ROE)			
		1986	1981	1982–1986		1977–1986	
				Mean	S.D.	Mean	S.D.
Alcan	7125.5	67000	66000	3.4	3.4	10.7	8.4
Northern Telecom	4525.5	46200	35400	18.2	2.3	15.7	5.7
Seagram (2)	3817.7	14400	16000	11.7	1.3	11.4	1.5
John Labatt (2)	3062.4	16200	9000	18.4	1.6	16.9	2.7
Gulf Canada	2410.6	17500	n/a	12.1	2.7	14.5	3.6
Noranda	3269.1	47600	79500	0.1	0.2	8.8	11.3
Moore	2572.1	27100	27700	15.4	1.9	16.5	1.8
Abitibi-Price (1)	2149.0	16200	17800	9.6	2.4	14.3	7.8
Nova	3429.0	7100	10000	10.2	0.9	10.9	4.1
MacMillan Bloedel	2172.1	15100	22100	4.9	5.7	8.9	8.1
Domtar	2001.6	15300	17400	10.3	6.2	12.5	6.2
Molson	1938.6	11300	13200	12.7	3.4	15.1	3.8
Consolidated-Bathurst	1637.0	14600	16000	10.0	2.6	15.1	7.4
Ivaco	1183.6	12000	7000	5.1	4.1	12.1	9.7
Varity	2011.6	19000	39800	0.7	0.9	0.7	1.3
AMCA International	1784.3	8900	21800	2.9	4.5	10.9	8.0
Inco	1801.3	20200	31700	1.1	2.2	4.0	4.6
Cominco	1395.2	8500	12600	0.5	0.9	9.4	10.8
Falconbridge	773.5	8900	15100	2.1	2.5	5.1	7.1
Bombardier	663.7	13000	7100	8.8	3.6	7.0	4.9
Canfor	977.0	5300	n/a	2.2	4.3	n/a	n/a
Magna International	389.0	10300	3000	18.2	5.0	20.5	6.6
Total	48678.8	404200	474800				
Average	2318.0	20210	23740	8.0	2.9	11.3	6.1

Notes: Gulf excluded from calculations because of change of ownership in 1985.
  (1) Data for ROE is a nine year average.
  (2) Employment figures are for 1986 and 1982

Source: Corporate Annual Reports, Financial Post 500 (various issues).
  Statistical Yearbook year end exchange rate.

advances or declines by the Canadian multinationals may
not represent permanent changes in their sales generating
capabilities.

The average sales of the Canadian multinationals is
Cdn. $2.3 billion. Compared to their international counter-
parts they are relatively small. The largest, Alcan, had 1986
sales of Cdn. $8.2 billion. The largest U.S. and European
multinational enterprises, General Motors, and Royal
Dutch/Shell have 1986 sales in excess of Cdn. $100 billion.
However, many of the Canadian multinationals are world
leaders, for example, Abitibi-Price in newsprint, Inco in
nickel, Seagram in distilled spirits, Cominco in lead and
zinc, and Moore in business forms.

The 22 Canadian-owned industrial enterprises employed
404,200 people or 4 percent of the Canadian employed work
force in 1986, with the average number of employees being
20,210. The employment figures include workers employed
in the foreign subsidiaries of these firms. The 1981–1983
recession resulted in a decline in employment for the majority of the corporations. Two companies suffered in particular—Inco which reduced its labour force by 11,500
between 1981 and 1986 and Varity which reduced its labour
force by 20,800 workers, over the same period. In contrast,
Northern Telecom swelled its rank of employees over the
same period by 10,800 from 35,400 to 46,200.

Finally, the successful financial performance of Canada's largest multinational enterprises can also be observed
in table 5.7. Over the last five years these 22 multinationals
earned an average return on equity of 8.0 percent and had a
standard deviation of 2.9 percent. Over the 10-year period
between 1977 and 1986 the 22 multinationals had an average ROE of 11.3 and SD of 6.1. These numbers demonstrate
the effect of the recession on the Canadian MNEs. The overall average was dragged down by the performance of Noranda, Inco, Varity, and Cominco during the recession. The
10-year standard deviation is higher than for the large U.S.
multinationals, reflecting the greater risk of the relatively
smaller and thinner financial markets and economic system in Canada compared to the United States. The mean
ROE is also lower than the profits of the large U.S. multinationals (reported in table 5.3 as 15.3 percent). Over roughly

the same period (1970–1983) the average ROE for European multinationals was only 8.5 percent, and for Japanese multinationals, 10.5 percent (Rugman and McIlveen 1985).

The implications of these data on the financial performance of Canada's largest multinationals is that they are worthy members of the billion dollar club. Over the last decade, even including the recession years of 1981–1983, these primarily mature and resource-based firms achieved a satisfactory financial performance. They were just as successful as the high-tech multinationals from the United States, Europe, and Japan. Most of the sales of these Canadian multinationals are in the United States. As U.S. non-tariff barriers to trade have escalated these Canadian-owned multinationals have retained access to this vital market, thereby generating economic benefits to Canadians in the forms of jobs, dividends and wealth transfers. With trade liberalization this tendency to outward direct investment may be slowed down but not reversed for reasons to be examined in the following chapters.

CHAPTER 6

Strategic Planning, Adjustment and Trade Liberalization*

THE STRATEGIC MANAGEMENT OF MULTINATIONAL ENTERPRISES

The manner in which multinational enterprises will adjust to trade liberalization measures, depends upon the decisions made by their key strategic planners. This involves the chief executive officer and his senior staff, working within general strategic guidelines usually determined by the executive committee of the board.

As is well known to scholars of management, the process of strategic planning follows patterns in which the competitive strengths of the firm are constantly reassessed in light of new information about the domestic and international environments within which the firm operates. Such environmental changes would include trade liberalization measures, to which the multinational enterprises would react. This process of competitive strategy has been synthesized most recently in works by Porter (1980, 1985). Applications in an international dimension are considered by Rugman (1985a) and Porter (1986). Here this thinking is applied in a new context, to discover the basic principles involved in reacting, at the firm level, to fundamental changes in the U.S.-Canadian trading relationship.

By definition, strategic management decisions take place under conditions of uncertainty and partial ignorance; consequently they cannot be easily understood nor programmed by the analyst. Investment decisions are especially important to model, since they help to determine the "competitive scope" of a firm, that is, its product-market domain. Foreign direct investment decisions of multinational enterprises are a special case, since they tend to re-

---

*This chapter is coauthored with Dr. Alain Verbeke.

sult from three critical decisions made by corporate management.

First, in spite of the extra costs of doing business abroad, the organization will be able to develop activities that will be competitive with the business activities of local firms, provided that it has a firm specific advantage (FSA). The FSA reflects the competitive strength of the company, whether this is derived from production (R & D based) or marketing (customization) advantages. Second, the net benefits resulting from the direct investment abroad are larger than the benefits that would result from exports or licensing agreements. Third, the chosen location for the development of production activities is the best possible one.

The three decisions above are the managerial equivalents of the eclectic model of Dunning (1981) who specifies three economic determinants of foreign direct investment, referred to respectively as ownership, internalization, and location advantages. These decisions are not made sequentially but simultaneously, with the second decision being the most crucial one. Dunning's theoretical framework from economics helps to explain the strategic investment behavior of multinational enterprises. His work is consistent with other theories investigating internalization by multinational enterprises, for example see Buckley and Casson (1976), Rugman (1981), and Dunning and Rugman (1985). Internalization is based on the idea developed by Coase (1937) that markets and hierarchical structures (firms) are alternatives: A product or service will be provided in-house (by a firm) if it can be produced at a cost less than that involved with an open market transaction.

Transaction costs associated with market contracting lead to internalization: the external environment is replaced by an internal market of the firm, making for an efficient international transfer of proprietary knowledge embodied in goods, materials, and people. In this way market contracting costs resulting from opportunism, bounded rationality, and asset specificity are prevented (Williamson 1975, 1985). The existence of externalities is an additional reason for internalization. With market imperfections such as the public goods nature of knowledge, or buyer uncertainty, there are reasons for internal markets of multinational enterprises to develop (Rugman 1981; Caves 1982; and Rugman, Lecraw, and Booth 1985).

In general, three types of foreign direct investment can be distinguished:

1. Horizontal integration investments, whereby plants of the multinational enterprise in different countries produce similar goods

2. Vertical integration investments, whereby plants of the multinational enterprise in different countries produce at adjacent stages of a vertically related set of production processes

3. Diversification investments, whereby the different plants produce different goods and need not be vertically related

Horizontally integrated multinational enterprises exist because of their greater overall enterprise-wide efficiency (synergy) as compared with the case whereby each plant would have separate management. Two factors can cause such managerial efficiency. The first one is due to scale economies in production (raw materials procurement, economies in transportation). The second, and more important reason, is the existence of FSAs in the form of intangible assets belonging to the multinational enterprise. These can be related to proprietary production (created by R & D) or to marketing skills. Intangible marketing-related assets refer to skills available in the multinational enterprise that generate a greater willingness to pay by consumers as compared to their attitudes towards purchasing comparable products of competitors. Marketing FSAs may take the form of promotion abilities, advertising, a trademark or a brand name. Both production and marketing FSAs can possibly generate economic rents and are crucial to the profitability and growth of the multinational enterprise.

A basic conceptual question is why firms prefer internalization and do not rent or sell their FSAs to other firms. The answer is that, because of market imperfections, single-plant firms cannot successfully rent or sell their intangible assets to other single-plant firms. To explain this Johnson (1970) and Magee (1977) developed the idea of appropriability. Organizations that possess a unique body of knowledge in the form of FSAs will try to keep this knowledge for themselves. This is the case with R & D knowledge for two reasons:

1. R & D costs can only be recovered as the result of benefits that flow to the organization over a long period of time

2. Technological "knowhow" is a public good: its use by other organizations does not limit the use by its initial owner, but it reduces the benefits flowing to this initial owner

This problem of appropriability partly explains why multinational enterprises exist: National companies prefer to transfer their technology within their own organization, rather than engaging in contracts with foreign firms and risking dissipation of their technological knowhow. The risk of dissipation and related transaction costs would be especially high whenever one or more of the five following factors holds:

1. The reputation or brand name of the company is very important for the consumer so that quality controls are crucial

2. After sales service is crucial

3. Complementarities exist between the different products manufactured by the firm so that internal production is most efficient

4. Products are new and differentiated; this results in an information asymmetry between seller and buyer

5. Diversification of production lines generates learning effects and a spread of risks

Williamson (1981, 1985) has investigated in some depth why multinational enterprises have the ability and choose to develop international production activities. Technological knowhow is considered as the main FSA of multinational enterprises. Williamson identifies different problems when technological knowhow is transferred abroad, without foreign direct investment. The two most important ones are the problem of "disclosure" and the problem of "team organization." The former refers to the so called fundamental paradox discovered by Arrow (1971): the value of information (knowhow) is unknown to its potential buyer until access to it is achieved, but at that moment the information has been acquired at no cost. This means that technological knowhow is often spread over a number of individuals, each of whom masters only part of it. In that case a contract for technology transfer is excluded and only the use of a consulting team or foreign direct investment constitute viable solutions; foreign direct investment will be chosen if transfer activities have to be performed continuously.

Apart from transaction costs (which will always be found in the presence of bounded rationality, opportunism, and asset specificity) and the natural market imperfections mentioned, which in turn can generate transaction costs, foreign direct investment can also be caused by unnatural market imperfections (Rugman 1981). The latter include government imposed imperfections in the form of tariff and non-tariff barriers. Such imperfections may increase the relative benefits associated with foreign direct investment, as compared with exports. This same observation holds for vertically integrated and diversified multinational enterprises.

Transactional reasons also constitute the main rationale for the existence of vertically integrated multinational enterprises; contracting costs and uncertainty lead to the internalization of markets for intermediate products. Buckley and Casson (1976) focused much of their attention on natural market imperfections in the markets for intermediate goods. This is a sufficient rationale for internalization. Intermediate goods may refer to technological knowhow, human capital, raw materials, and semi-finished goods. Imperfections in these markets lead to internalization; control of the activities involved by business firms.

Natural market imperfections can arise due to:

1. The impossibility of developing long-term contracts for certain goods
2. The impossibility of engaging in price-discrimination
3. The danger of opportunistic behavior by the party with whom a contractual agreement is signed, especially in the case of a bilateral concentration of market power
4. The existence of "information asymmetry" between buyer and seller, such as buyer uncertainty (when the buyer wishes to pay too low a price for a good, because the information to assess its real value is lacking)

In any of the cases mentioned above, internalization may also lead to the creation of rents resulting from FSAs. Teece (1982) has argued that vertical integration investments would take place, whenever "specific assets" create a strong mutual dependence between two economic actors (such as the existence of fixed assets that cannot be used in a profitable way for other purposes) and opportunistic behavior by one of the actors would lead to high costs for the other actor. In this case vertical integration prevents high transaction costs associated with market contracting (including enforcement and control costs).

Diversified multinational enterprises are the third category of multinational enterprises; their existence can be explained by the risk diversification hypothesis (Rugman 1979). The management of multinational enterprises is assumed to be risk averse; attempts are made to reduce the variability of the firm's rate of return on equity capital. As economic disturbances in different countries are often less than perfectly positively correlated, foreign direct investment can lead to risk reduction. Here again the competitive strengths of the multinational enterprises in comparison to national competitors flow from its FSAs.

Economic rents, however, can also flow from country specific advantages (CSAs). The CSAs capture the natural factor endowments of a nation, basically the variables in its aggregate production function. CSAs are related to inputs in terms of their quality, quantity, and costs relative to other countries. They can also include the political-cultural systems and governmental variables of different nations. For a discussion of the fundamentals of this theory see Rugman (1980a) and Rugman, Lecraw, and Booth (1985).

In models of strategic management both categories of advantages (FSAs and CSAs) can influence the structure of competition and the attractiveness of the strategic options open to firms, especially multinational enterprises. It is important to recognize that CSAs are best assumed to be exogeneous parameters for the firm, while the FSAs are endogenous and have been developed by the firm, such as special knowhow or a core skill, that is unavailable to others and cannot be duplicated by them, except in the long run and at high cost. An important objective of the management of the internal market of a firm is to establish and retain property rights over the FSAs, so that they cannot be dissipated to other firms.

CSAs include tariffs, non-tariff barriers and other government barriers to trade, including regulations on foreign direct investment. If such unnatural market imperfections change or are eliminated this may affect industry competition. Such changes influence both the level of transaction costs that multinational enterprises are confronted with in the international environment and the shelter they have obtained from global competitive pressures. In this connection the process of trade liberalization can be regarded as the removal of such governmental impediments to international competition.

For the internationally competitive operations of multinational enterprises, the impact of a free trade area will be positive. Its main effects will be to reduce transaction costs associated with exports and to create more certainty for investment decisions. Both of these factors enhance market access and efficient production, thereby stimulating employment opportunities. In cases where foreign direct investment and exports are complements, a free trade area may increase the level of both. A substitution of exports for foreign direct investment can be expected in cases where unnatural market imperfections were the main rationale for engaging in foreign direct investment and where exit barriers are low, so that adjustment costs of relocating production activities are limited.

Two important conclusions can be drawn from the analysis made above. First, a change in trade barriers should not necessarily have an important effect on strategic management decisions in multinational enterprises. Unnatural market imperfections represent only some of the variables taken into account by their strategic planners. The transaction costs resulting from natural market imperfections are not affected at all by a free trade area. Second, in cases where unnatural market imperfections are important variables in strategic management decisions, strategic planners will try to minimize adjustment costs faced by the multinational enterprise after the introduction of a free trade area.

Moreover, the creation of this free trade area will generate benefits in terms of a more stable environment (decrease of uncertainty and partial ignorance) so that Canadian and U.S. multinationals will be able to integrate their operations more efficiently in both countries (Aho and Levinson 1987).

THE NATURE OF COMPETITIVE STRATEGY

This section demonstrates how multinational enterprises attempt to turn their CSAs and FSAs into economic rents, through the use of competitive strategies. Porter (1980) has argued that firms can develop three, internally consistent, generic strategies, namely: overall cost leadership, differentiation, and focus.

Achieving overall cost leadership requires an organizational emphasis upon the cost control of inputs and a production process that allows firms to obtain economies of scale and experience curve effects. The differentiation strategy, on the contrary, requires the creation of products and services that are perceived as unique by customers and emphasizes marketing aspects to gain competitive advantages. Focus, the third generic strategy, is aimed at serving a particular segment of the market, such as a narrow geographic area, a well-defined buyer group, or a limited product line. The competitive strengths of a firm engaging in the focus strategy also rest on the ability to achieve low cost or differentiation but only vis-à-vis the chosen market segment. This strategy by definition limits the overall market-share that is achievable but may still allow an above average profitability.

Some firms are not successful in any of these three generic strategies: if a firm fails to achieve overall cost leadership, industry wide differentiation, or focus in a particular market segment, it becomes "stuck in the middle," which is in the long run, a guarantee for low profitability, especially in industries that are (or become) globally competitive.

Porter's model is strongly related to internalization theory with the latter's focus upon FSAs and CSAs for the multinational enterprise. Each of the three generic strategies should be seen as a set of defensive or offensive actions, aimed at deriving rents from the CSAs and FSAs of the multinational enterprise. Whether the structure of competition in an industry will be strongly affected by a free trade area between two countries depends on entry and exit barriers, in addition to the CSAs and FSAs of the firms involved.

Entry barriers refer to the difficulties that potential entrants face when trying to enter an industry. The seven key entry barriers identified by Porter (1980, 1985) are: economies of scale, product differentiation, capital requirements, switching costs, distribution channels, cost disadvantages independent of scale, and government policy.

Economies of scale refer to decreases in unit costs of a product as its absolute volume in one period rises. A particular type of economies of scale is created when business units, in a multinational enterprise, share intangible assets that can be transferred at negligible costs between the different units. Another type consists of economies of vertical integration, which may leave non-integrated competitors with a cost disadvantage, such as when integrated firms control the supply of certain inputs and demand higher prices for these inputs when selling to outside firms. Product differentiation creates customer loyalties and brand identification. In order to break such a barrier, competitors may have to engage in high and risky marketing expenses. Sometimes, huge capital requirements exist in order to build the necessary production facilities, cover start-up losses, fulfill the needs for working-capital, etc. Switching costs refer to costs faced by buyers to substitute a new supplier for an existing one (such costs may also be encountered by suppliers of a good). These costs do not only include adaptation problems to new equipment but also uncertainty and psychic costs. Access to distribution channels is of great importance; if major distribution channels are completely tied up by existing competitors it may become extremely difficult for new entrants to market their products, unless new distribution channels are created. New firms may suffer from cost disadvantages independent of scale vis-à-vis established firms which may enjoy proprietary knowledge and experience curve effects, economies of location, advantageous access to raw materials. Government policy includes explicit and implicit barriers to entry. Explicit barriers involve the regulation of an industry, in terms of determining the number of producers and market structure, raising international trade barriers, etc. Implicit barriers may result from market imperfections in the form of externalities (e.g., restrictions on pollution may increase capital requirements for potential entrants).

The important question for adjustment within the Canadian economy is whether the introduction of a free trade area will result in:

1. A status quo, because the decrease in entry barriers (in this case the equivalent of government regulation) for a multinational enterprise is insufficient to allow entry in Canada

2. New entries of multinational enterprises, because the decrease in entry barriers is so substantial that it provides the economic impetus for entry in Canada

3. A rise in entry barriers, because existing firms can now expand and profit from, e.g., economies of scale and experience curve effects

It is clear that a status quo or a rise in entry barriers will be the dominating effect of a free trade area on the Canadian economy. A status quo will be observed in all industries where the elimination of unnatural market imperfections has negligible effects on investment or export decisions of foreign multinational enterprises. A rise in entry barriers can be expected in industries where efficient Canadian multinationals can increase entry barriers for foreign competitors by exploiting economies of scale in serving the much larger American market through exports instead of foreign direct investment. The potential for new entries of foreign multinational enterprises competing with Canadian firms will be limited, since the introduction of a free trade area will only influence the relative benefits associated with foreign direct investment and exports, but not the barriers to entry in the Canadian marketplace.

Exit barriers are important for multinational enterprises which will be confronted with a weaker competitive position in certain operations, after a free trade agreement is reached. The main question is then whether decreased profits will result in divestment. Six exit barriers may prevent a firm from leaving the market: durable and specialized

assets, fixed costs of exit, strategic exit barriers, information barriers, managerial or emotional barriers, government
and social barriers.

Durable and specialized assets refer to assets that cannot be liquidated except at very low prices. Fixed costs of
exit, are related to costs of labour settlements, cancellation
penalties for breaking long-term contracts and the deterio-
ration of a firm's strengths vis-à-vis its environment. Strategic exit barriers include: (a) the interrelations of the
declining business with other businesses and its importance for the image of the corporation; (b) the negative impact a divestment would have on the access to financial
markets. An incremental divestment, spread over a number
of years, may then be warranted so as to prevent a reduction
of the financial credibility of the firm; (c) vertical relations
of the business with other units in the company. Information barriers exist when a business is strongly related to
other ones in a firm or shares common resources or assets
so that its real performance may be very difficult to assess
and hence appropriate exit decisions may not be taken.
Managerial or emotional barriers are related to "commitment" to the business involved. These barriers may even
extend to top management of diversified firms. Government
and social barriers include explicit or implicit pressure exerted by non-market actors so that economically justified
exit decisions are prevented.

Exit barriers determine how multinational enterprises
will react when losing important CSAs in certain businesses, as a result of a free trade area. With respect to exit
barriers, a free trade agreement may have two different effects on businesses in a multinational enterprise that lose
their CSAs:

    1. Exit, because of low exit barriers
    2. Status quo (maintaining business with low profitability)
because of high exit barriers.

THE GLOBAL MATRIX AND STRATEGIES OF MULTINATIONALS

To understand the manner in which multinational enterprises can respond to trade liberalization we need a conceptual framework that binds together national and

enterprise influences on global strategic management and economic planning. This can be achieved by combining in a new matrix the national CSAs with the enterprise-level FSAs. This is demonstrated in figure 6.1 where the horizontal axis measures FSAs and the vertical axis captures the CSAs. It should be emphasized that this matrix does not include CSAs resulting from protectionism and trade barriers.

The conceptual basis for this matrix can be found in Rugman (1981) and Rugman, Lecraw, and Booth (1985). In these works on the theory of the multinational enterprise and its application in the field of international business, the distinction was drawn between CSAs as environmental parameters, and FSAs as managerial decision variables. The FSAs reflect the competitive strengths of the company, as explained earlier in this chapter. The CSAs are environmental parameters for the strategic planners of a firm in a small nation such as Canada, but it is conceivable that they

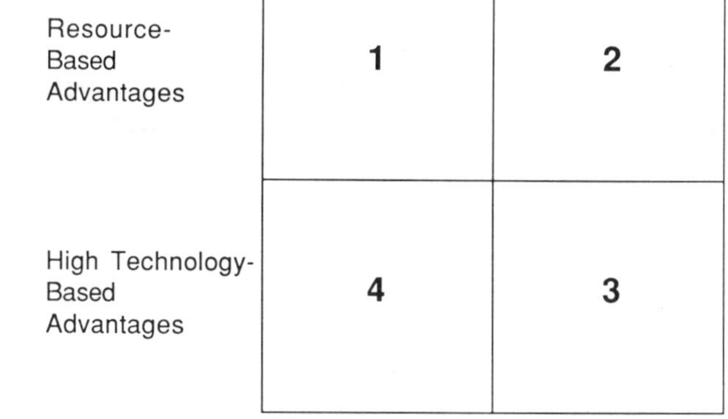

	Production-Oriented	Marketing-Oriented
Resource-Based Advantages	1	2
High Technology-Based Advantages	4	3

Firm-Specific Advantages

Country-Specific Advantages

Figure 6.1   The Placement of the World's Largest MNE's in the Global Matrix

are variables for those who believe in industrial policies
and other measures that can generate a "man-made" comparative advantage in larger nations such as the United
States. The distinction between CSAs and FSAs is now discussed more specifically. The CSA axis captures the natural
factor endowments of a nation and reflects the economic
theory of comparative advantage of nations. The axis is di-
vided into resource-based and technology-intensive segments, with the former in the upper half. For some
purposes the resource-based sector can also be thought
of as "low technology" and the other sector as "high technology."

To an extent, but not necessarily to an important degree, these natural comparative advantages can be shifted
by industrial policies. Some of the newly industrialized
countries have developed a "man-made" CSA in the high
technology area (and this would appear in the lower part of
this axis). However, such movements are extremely difficult
to accomplish, especially in a short period of time, so that
the division between resource-based and technology-based
comparative advantages is the basic one for policy analysis.
With this caveat incorporated on the CSA axis is this concept of state support for business. Towards the top of the
vertical CSA axis the role of government is small. Here "natural" competitive advantage is paramount, with relative factor endowments being the source of a nation's comparative
advantage. Towards the bottom of the axis the role of the
state increases, such that a "man-made" or "artificial"
comparative advantage can result. Here the state supports
business to the extent that international competitiveness
can be switched away from natural factor endowments towards high-technology areas. This has already occurred in
Japan and some of the Asian NICs, but not in oil-rich Arab
nations.

The FSA axis is functionally determined by the broad
characteristics of enterprise structure. It moves horizontally from a production-based FSA on the left, towards a
marketing-based service FSA on the right. Production FSAs
are basically "hardware" advantages at the firm level, reflecting efficient cost minimizing economic decisions. Enterprise strategies will be low cost and price based. Some

firms achieve production FSAs through vertical integration, the use of process technology, and economies of scale. At the other extreme on this axis, marketing FSAs reflect "software" advantages. These are micro management skills in the organization of human resources, customization, cooperative relationships with suppliers and customers, marketing networks, and control over the channels of distribution. Enterprise strategies to the right of the FSA axis involve overall differentiation or focus differentiation, based upon the gathering of customized intelligence.

The horizontal dimension of the FSA axis also measures the "economies of scope" enjoyed by firms able to combine these hardware and software skills. By economies of scope is meant the ability of an enterprise to achieve per unit cost reductions as it increases output of closely related, but distinctive, product lines. Thus, economies of scope arise when the manufacture of customized product lines, determined by marketing intelligence, can benefit from scale economies achieved by the use of modular sub-assemblies which are quickly adaptable to product variants.

Using this matrix, the world's largest 200 multinational enterprises, (Stopford 1982), can be positioned in their current strategic spaces. Most of the U.S. and European multinational enterprises are in quadrant 4 of figure 6.1 where they compete on production-based FSAs building on high-technology CSAs. This is the area for Vernon's product cycle multinational enterprises, where competitive ability rests on R & D to discover and commercialize new product lines. However, spanning quadrants 4 and 3 are a group of Japanese multinational enterprises who combine product and marketing skills. They utilize economies of scope whereby they incorporate marketing intelligence with the ability to use sub-assemblies and flexible manufacturing systems on the production side.

The problems of the production-based approach can be visualized by considering multinational enterprises competing in quadrants 1 and 2. In quadrant 1, a group of third world multinational enterprises (backed by their governments) are now the low cost producers. However, recent research by Rugman and McIlveen (1985) demonstrates that Canadian resource-based multinational enterprises are now operating in quadrant 2 rather than in 1. The Canadian resource-based multinational enterprises have developed a value-added chain in the harvesting, processing and marketing of resource and mature product lines. The lesson is that marketing skills can help even resource-based multinational enterprises to compete globally.

In terms of public policy it should be noted that national strategies need to recognize the strategic attributes of the home multinational enterprises located in the country. There is no reason why industrial policy should always focus only upon quadrant 4, as most of the literature advocates. Instead, nations should consider the benefits of strategies that would move their multinational enterprises into quadrants where there is a better mix of CSAs and FSAs. In this manner national policy would build upon enterprise strategy.

In the Canadian context, multinational enterprises have developed mainly as a result of natural CSAs. The introduction of a free trade area between Canada and the United States will allow them to exploit their natural CSAs further, without a substantial influence being exerted on their production operations.

Figure 6.1 also allows us to observe that most Canadian multinational enterprises pursue a differentiation strategy. It should be considered as a focus differentiation strategy rather than an overall differentiation strategy, however, since the segment scope (the number of market segments served in an industry) of most firms is rather limited. The fact that most Canadian multinational enterprises pursue focus differentiation strategies is extremely important. The elimination of unnatural market imperfections will not substantially decrease the main entry barriers that foreign competitors face, namely product differentiation, buyer switching costs, and access to distribution channels.

In order to predict the influence of trade liberalization on competitive strategies of business firms, figure 6.1 must be extended for two reasons. First, it only reflects the efficient operations of resource-based Canadian multinational enterprises and not operations of other types of firms. Second, it does not describe the effect of a change in unnatural market imperfections on CSAs and thus on the strategies of business firms. In the next section, a new framework is developed to perform such an analysis.

Application of the structure/conduct/performance model of industrial organization to the Canadian situation was undertaken by Caves et al. (1980). They analyzed the key economic determinants of competition and foreign investment in the Canadian economy, but did not use the managerial framework of this chapter.

TRADE LIBERALIZATION AND COMPETITIVE STRATEGY

In the context of Canadian trade policy, the impact of a free trade area can be studied for different types of firms. This section will focus especially on two specific categories of firms:

1. Operations of Canadian multinationals in Canada
2. Subsidiaries of U.S. multinationals in Canada

The question is how the introduction of a free trade area will influence the investment behavior of these two categories of multinational enterprises. Conceptually, for any business of a firm we can analyze whether Canada possesses strong or weak CSAs and whether this business benefits from strong or weak FSAs.

Any business can then be placed in one of the quadrants of figure 6.2. This diagram presents a classification of the businesses in which a firm competes in terms of the strengths of CSAs and FSAs. International competitiveness is assured whenever FSAs and CSAs are strong simultaneously (quadrant 1). If CSAs are weak, however, FSAs will have to be very substantial, in order to compete with global rivals (quadrant 4). A similar observation holds in case a firm does not possess strong FSAs; then only through CSAs can a strong competitive position be assured (quadrant 2). For businesses where both CSAs and FSAs are lacking or restricted, competing internationally with efficient foreign rivals is made very difficult (quadrant 3).

A free trade agreement will have different effects on different categories of businesses in figure 6.2 in terms of investment behavior. The potential responses of business firms to a free trade area are outlined in figure 6.3, and will now be explained.

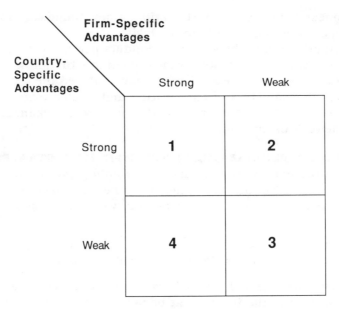

Figure 6.2   The Competitive Advantage Matrix

1. For those businesses located in quadrant 1 for which a free trade agreement has little effect, or where it constitutes primarily a decrease in trade barriers and hence a stronger competitive position in the free trade area, the potential effects will be an increase in domestic investment and some substitution of exports for foreign direct investment. Such a situation can be expected for most Canadian resource-based multinationals, especially in global industries, whereby FSAs and CSAs not relevant to protection guarantee international competitiveness. Examples include firms in the pulp and paper industry (Abitibi-Price, Consolidated-Bathurst, Domtar, and MacMillan Bloedel), and in the mining and metals industry (Noranda, Alcan, and Cominco).

The same observation holds for subsidiaries of foreign multinational enterprises with world product mandates (WPMs) or globally rationalized businesses. Both categories of subsidiaries possess strong FSAs of their parents that allow them to compete efficiently on an international scale. A WPM can be defined as the full development, production,

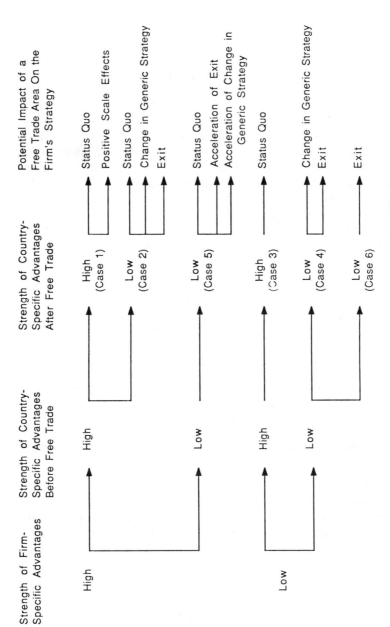

Figure 6.3 Strategic Responses to Trade Liberalization

and marketing of a new product line in a subsidiary of a multinational enterprise (Rugman 1983a). At present WPMs are restricted to mainly vertically integrated multinational enterprises that operate in Canada to take advantage of its natural resources. WPMs based on the processing and marketing of Canadian resources in the areas of minerals, forestry, agriculture, food processing, and other related areas are common examples. Globally rationalized businesses typically produce only a limited fraction of the total product line of a multinational enterprise for the world market. Unlike subsidiaries with WPMs they are essentially production driven and concentrate on low costs.

With respect to branch plants of foreign multinational enterprises in Canada, three categories should be distinguished:

   a. Branch plants that can only be economically sustained because of unnatural market imperfections (the so called "tariff factories," see MacCharles [1986]) and face low exit barriers

   b. Branch plants that were set up primarily because of unnatural market imperfections, but will remain viable after a free trade agreement because of strong FSAs of the parent firm or be restructured because of high exit barriers (change of competitive scope)

   c. Branch plants that were set up for other reasons than government induced market imperfections (as described in the first section of this chapter) and which will keep their competitive advantages after a free trade area is installed

Most of the larger subsidiaries of U.S. multinational enterprises, for example those studied in chapter 5, fall in this third category of branch plants (automobile sector, oil sector, distribution, etc.). These subsidiaries are internationally competitive firms that derive their competitive strengths from the FSA of their U.S. parent.

2. For those businesses located in quadrant 1 for which the free trade area constitutes primarily a decrease in shelter, there is a decrease in CSAs and a shift to the fourth quadrant; there are three likely responses. First, a status quo because strong FSAs combined with high exit barriers compensate for the decline in CSAs. Second, restructuring, a major change in generic strategy. Third, relocation of ac-

tivities (exit, depending upon exit barriers). The last two cases will be primarily applicable to a limited set of subsidiaries of U.S. multinational enterprises; those that were set up to serve the Canadian market because of the high costs associated with exports, but are of inefficient scale to compete successfully in a free trade area. Only if exit barriers are low will a relocation of activities be carried out (first category of branch plants).

In the case of high exit barriers, a change in generic strategy may be necessary to maintain profitability. Strategies of overall cost leadership or differentiation that could be successfully pursued in the Canadian context, before the introduction of a free trade area, cannot be sustained in a more global environment. Then a focus strategy becomes necessary. This may take the form of global rationalization, whereby the product scope of the subsidiary is restricted. FSAs of the parent company then make international competitiveness possible (second category of branch plants).

It is apparent, however, that none of the subsidiaries of U.S. multinational enterprises, analyzed in chapter 5 of this study, fall into the first or second category of branch plants. This is consistent with the observation that the successive reductions in protective tariffs as a result of the different GATT negotiations after the Second World War have not generated any substantial withdrawals of U.S. subsidiaries from Canada. Changes in strategy may be necessary, however, for certain operations of Canadian multinational enterprises where unnatural market imperfections (such as protected markets) were an important factor for success. Some firms in the beverage industry, such as Labatt and Molson, fit into this category.

3. For those businesses located in quadrant 2 for which the free trade area constitutes primarily a decrease in trade barriers, but which will not expand because of weak FSAs, there are no effects on investment behavior. This quadrant is primarily applicable not to multinational enterprises but to businesses of local Canadian firms that do not face global competitive pressures from foreign firms, because of the multidomestic character of the industry or because a nationally responsive strategy as described by Porter (1986) constitutes a viable focus strategy. Examples occur in the

resource-based sectors where production is mainly for domestic consumption, such as in fish, forestry, some agriculture and related areas which do not depend on marketing boards for protection. This quadrant may, however, also describe a limited set of operations of Canadian multinational enterprises, especially in mature industries, where FSAs have been eroded over time by competitive strategies of efficient foreign rivals, so that a free trade area does not constitute an important market opportunity.

4. For those businesses located in quadrant 2 for which the free trade area constitutes primarily a decrease in CSAs, firms will be either forced to divest or to restructure their businesses in Canada (a change in generic strategy). This is again a case of the inefficient local Canadian producers that were sheltered from foreign competition through trade barriers, but which must now shift to the third quadrant where they may be forced to exit, depending upon exit barriers, unless they are able to adopt a focus strategy that can be sustained against competition. Examples occur in the feather, egg, dairy, and related industries protected by marketing boards. In all these cases, both exit barriers for local firms and entry barriers for efficient foreign competitors are low. As protective mechanisms such as marketing boards were kept, and hence excluded from the free trade agreement, such businesses can survive. It may also apply to certain operations of Canadian multinational enterprises that were only economically viable, because of a protected Canadian market in the food and beverage industry.

5. For those businesses already in quadrant 4 the free trade area may have the effect of accelerating relocation to countries with high CSAs. This case is similar to case 2 above. It can be expected however that multinational enterprises in this quadrant already have diversified their geographic scope and/or will not be affected at all by a free trade area: Seagram and Hiram-Walker in the beverage industry and Moore in the technologically intensive information systems industry are examples.

6. For those businesses already in quadrant 3 for which the introduction of free trade could speed up the divestment process, this quadrant basically describes inefficient operations of any type of firm: multinational enterprises or

local firms. Exit will again depend upon exit barriers. Certain types of operations and firms, such as Massey-Ferguson, may fall into this quadrant.

An important issue of adjustment to examine, is how these impacts on investment behavior are related to Porter's generic strategy types. For Canadian operations of Canadian multinational enterprises and subsidiaries of U.S. multinational enterprises that were located in quadrant 1 of figure 6.2 before the free trade area and that make up the bulk of firms analyzed in this study, three alternative courses of action (apart from exit as in case 2) exist:

1. No change in strategy, but a possible increase of investment in Canada in order to capture scale effects, as a result of the larger market (case 1, quadrant 1 of figure 6.2). This adjustment may generate a rise in entry barriers for potential entrants.

2. Change of generic strategy in the operations located in Canada, from overall cost leadership or differentiation, in the Canadian context, toward a focus strategy in the larger free trade area (case 2, quadrant 1).

3. Change in generic strategy by modifying the competitive scope, starting from a focus strategy (case 2, quadrant 1). Four dimensions are characteristic of competitive scope: segment scope, geographic scope, industry scope, and vertical scope. Segment scope refers to the range of market segments served by the firm in terms of categories of buyers and product varieties. Geographic scope is related to the extent of the geographic market in which the firm competes. Vertical scope refers to the degree of vertical integration by the firm. Industry scope refers to the number of businesses in which the firm competes. A change in competitive scope may be accompanied by substantial adjustment costs for the companies involved.

FREE TRADE AND U.S. SUBSIDIARIES IN CANADA

It is particularly important to study the probable managerial adjustments likely to be made by U.S. subsidiaries in Canada to the advent of trade liberalization. This section explores the adjustments likely to be made by different categories of U.S. subsidiaries. Again these strategies are explored within the framework of modern management theory.

Of particular relevance is the concept of the "value chain," introduced by Porter (1985). It describes the firm's total range of activities and it can be used to assess how firms achieve low costs, become differentiated or adopt focus strategies. The activities performed by any firm are classified for every business unit into nine generic categories: five of them include primary activities and four relate to support activities.

The primary activities consist of inbound logistics, operations, outbound logistics (all related to the physical creation of a product), marketing and sales, and service. The secondary activities are those involved in the procurement of purchased inputs, product and process technology development, human resource management, and infrastructure. Firm infrastructure is a very broad category of activities and encompasses such distinct functions as strategic management, finance, and accounting. The different categories of activities in a firm's value chain are interdependent. In order to gain competitive advantages the linkages between the different activities are extremely important.

With respect to structure, Porter (1986) makes a distinction between configuration and coordination issues. Configuration problems are related to the location in the world where the different activities in the value chain are performed. In the area of configuration, choices open to any firm range from concentration (whereby every activity in the value chain is performed in only one country) to dispersion (whereby an activity is performed in every country). The most extreme form of dispersion implies that every country has a complete value chain. Coordination on the other hand refers to how the activities of the firm (which may be dispersed or concentrated) are coordinated. Coordination may range from non-existing (full autonomy for each plant) to very tight (e.g., reciprocal interdependence, sharing of procedures and standards, continuous transfers of knowhow). A global strategy is then defined as "one in which a firm seeks to gain competitive advantage from its configuration, coordination among dispersed activities, or both" (Porter 1986).

Tariffs, non-tariff barriers and nationalistic purchasing may be thought of as a force for dispersing activities (Porter 1986) which is consistent with internalization theory as developed in the first section of this chapter. The creation of a free trade area on the other hand is an element working in favour of concentration of activities characterized by economies of scale and a proprietary learning curve. The location of these activities will depend on the respective CSAs of the nations involved, the coordination advantages of co-locating linked activities such as R & D and production, and exit barriers accompanying changes in configuration. Within a single firm, the advantage of concentrating an activity may be different for each activity in the value chain.

The main issue for adjustment purposes is whether a free trade area favours the concentration of the activities performed by different types of subsidiaries according to the activities they perform in the value chain. Alternatively, with respect to the coordination of dispersed activities, when a branch plant has autonomy, increasing globalization may lead to a decrease in independence and a stronger integration of the plant in a global network. In cases where a free trade area implies that subsidiaries will be faced with common customers or competitors in both countries, the need for vertical coordination will increase (vertical coordination refers to activities involving the subsidiary business unit with the corresponding business unit at the parent level).

The difference between this analysis and the traditional theory of comparative advantage is that here CSAs do not necessarily apply to the whole value chain of a business, but may be related to any generic category of activities. Comparative advantages in different stages in a vertically integrated industry sector, such as aluminum, may be located in different countries. Alcan performs bauxite mining in resource-rich countries, such as Brazil and Australia, while smelting will be found in countries with low electrical power cost, such as Canada (Stuckey 1983). This thinking can be extended within the value chain at any stage, so that the optimal location for performing individual activities may vary as well (Porter 1986).

In order to examine in more depth the possible adjustment policies of U.S. subsidiaries to trade liberalization, we consider the framework of D'Cruz (1986). He has made a distinction between six types of subsidiaries of multinational enterprises in Canada according to their decision making autonomy and the extent of their market involvement (see figure 6.4).

These six categories of subsidiaries can be linked to the value chain concept of Porter (1985) (see figure 6.5). Here, the degree of decision making autonomy is translated in terms of impact on "infrastructure" activities (low or high), while the extent of market involvement is referred to as geographic scope (national, limited international, world). Import businesses typically are reduced to importing products from the United States; their activities in the value chain emphasize marketing and sales. Satellite businesses, which are responsible for final assemblies, perform a limited part of operations and outbound logistics, in addition to marketing and sales. They will be found primarily in industries where low cost strategies dominate and final assemblies in Canada allow the firm to achieve cost reduction. Local service businesses, on the contrary, are characteristic of industries that face non-price competition, so that it becomes very important to perform local service activities in order to differentiate the firm's products (by providing a network of service outlets and service support to wholesalers and retailers). In this case the focus is on service, marketing and sales with substantial autonomy in these activities.

Decision-Making Autonomy

		Low	High
Extent of Market Involvement	World	Globally Rationalized	World Product Mandate
	North America	Satellite	Branch Plant
	Canada Only	Imports	Local Service

Figure 6.4   The Subsidiary Mission Grid
Source: Joseph R. D'Crus, "Strategic Management of Subsidiaries," in: Hamid Etemad and Louise Seguin Dulude, Managing the Multinational Subsidiary *(London and Signey: Croom Helm, 1986): 75–101.*

	Geographic Scope	Impact on Infrastructure Activities
Import Business	National	Low
Satellite Business	Limited International	Low
Local Service Business	National	High
Branch Plant	Limited International	High
Globally Rationalized Subsidiary	World	Low
World Product Mandate	World	High

Figure 6.5   A Re-Classification of Subsidiaries

The branch plants were classified into three categories in the previous section of this chapter. It was argued that only the first two categories are a response by foreign firms to government-imposed trade barriers, which have led to the development of relatively inefficient (small scale) operations suited to the Canadian market. The viability of these firms to carry out all the activities in the value chain (small tariff factories) may depend on the protection by barriers against foreign imports (first category). In these cases the inefficient production operations in the value chain can lead to an uncompetitive cost structure in cases where trade barriers are eliminated.

When a free trade area is installed, the viability of these U.S. branch plants in Canada (the country with the smaller market) may become endangered. The two most likely responses of strategic planners in these multinational enterprises (quadrant 1, case 2 in figure 6.2) are exit from Canada (change in configuration, depending upon exit barriers) or integration in a global network (this requires a change in coordination, and a possible change in configuration). Hence, some substitution of globally rationalized businesses for branch plants can be expected, especially in the long run. This alternative means the replacement of miniature replicas by firms that are more market driven. More efficient production subsidiaries will emerge, focused on a narrower competitive scope and taking advantage of scale economies and lower factor costs. Capital investment will be required to transform the plants to such specialized production.

However, only a limited number of branch plants will lose their competitive advantages after a free trade area. The third category of branch plant, which is neglected by D'Cruz, will continue its existing miniature replica approach, defined as "a firm producing roughly the same product line as its parent but at higher cost because of the small size of the market it services" (Bishop and Crookell 1983). Such branch plants can be extremely successful in manufacturing and marketing products according to procedures that have already succeeded in the United States; for this reason they can be cost competitive in Canada with broad product lines and even export. They are not truncated at all, nor completely dependent on parent competencies in the area of technology. In fact they receive strong competitive advantages from a continuous technology transfer resulting from the multinational development of their parent FSAs. This is true especially in industries where scale economies are limited or where activities other than operations are important in the value chain, and entry barriers are high. Then these U.S. subsidiaries may remain successful after a free trade agreement (case 1, quadrant 1 in figure 6.2).

Daly and MacCharles (1983) observed that in the 1970s the smaller Canadian subsidiaries (with less than 50 employees) of foreign firms were 50 percent more productive than Canadian controlled firms in the manufacturing sector (where productivity is expressed as value added per production worker). Only for larger firms (with more than 400 employees) no differences in productivity were observed.

Finally, the observation should be made that, even in the event of inefficient operation activities (first category), branch plants can be transformed into import businesses, whereby marketing and sales activities would be maintained in Canada.

In globally rationalized businesses, the emphasis is on operations. As concerns technology development and strategic planning, decision autonomy is even more limited than in branch plants. Typically, operations will be restricted to one stage of the production process for which the production facility aims at being a low cost producer for the world market. Installing globally rationalized operations is one way of transforming inefficient branch plants into an efficient subsidiary, after the elimination of trade barriers. Such changes cannot be expected to be implemented immediately. Doz and Prahalad (1981) reported that, in cases of a tradition of subsidiary self-sufficiency and autonomy, three years were necessary on average for corporate headquarters in a MNE to successfully gain control over subsidiary strategies and to implement global strategies.

Subsidiaries with world product mandates are the only ones that perform all activities in the value added chain, including technology development and strategic management. However, it has been observed by Crookell and Caliendo (1980), Rugman (1983a), and McGuinness and Conway (1986) that world product mandates have to be earned by the subsidiary and will not be routinely granted by the parent. Such mandates will not easily be earned, especially in high tech industries, where the parent would face high costs of transferring intangible intermediate knowledge products within existing production facilities from the United States to Canada. Only when Canada possesses strong CSAs can such a move be expected (Rugman and Douglas 1986). Moreover, new high technology businesses are usually located close to corporate headquarters in order to retain effective strategic decision making and generate faster communication for critical decisions about technology development.

A free trade area should not exert any significant influence on subsidiaries with world product mandates nor on businesses that are already globally rationalized. The relative costs of the activities of these firms compared to rival firms will not be affected by an elimination of unnatural market imperfections. This also holds for import and satellite businesses that were set up for efficiency reasons in Canada, irrespective of unnatural market imperfections, and for local service businesses that pursue specific focus strategies.

This chapter has extended prior work on competitive strategy to analyze the adjustment process of multinationals in a free-trade environment. A new framework was developed to assess the strategic planning decisions of the

Canadian multinationals and the U.S. subsidiaries. An important conclusion of the analysis is that the adjustment process depends upon the nature of the subsidiary and its firm-specific advantage. In general, efficient Canadian and U.S. subsidiaries should experience no difficulty in adjusting to the new free-trade environment. The theoretical results of this chapter are tested in the next chapter with surveys of the firms in the "billion dollar club."

CHAPTER 7

How Multinationals Will Respond to Trade Liberalization

QUESTIONNAIRE SAMPLE AND DESIGN

A questionnaire was administered to gather data on the viewpoint of senior management towards the adjustment process following trade liberalization. The entire set of 21 Canadian multinationals plus the group of the 22 largest U.S. subsidiaries in Canada, identified in chapter 5, were included in the work.

The questionnaire was sent to the chief executive officer of each Canadian multinational enterprise and each U.S. subsidiary in Canada, with the following exceptions. Genstar Corporation was acquired by Imasco in 1986, and most of the component companies of Genstar had been sold off by 1987. Therefore, it was deleted from the survey. Hiram Walker Resources was acquired by Gulf in 1986 and its return was organized by Gulf. In addition, Gulf submitted a separate response from its new subsidiary, Consumer Gas. Thus the total number of Canadian-owned multinationals involved was 21. By a similar process the questionnaire was sent to the 22 U.S. subsidiaries identified in chapter 5. Responses from the five retailers included in the list of the 22 U.S. subsidiaries indicated that they were not interested in participating so they were eliminated. This decision reflects the nature of their business in Canada, which primarily involves wholesaling, distribution, and the retailing of products in Canada. These firms included: Sears, Canada Safeway, F. W. Woolworth, K-Mart, and Great A & P Co. These types of retailing firms are not as concerned about adjustment issues as the 17 manufacturing subsidiaries left in the billion dollar club.

The questionnaire itself was designed to elicit information on the attitude of these senior managers towards both a comprehensive bilateral trade agreement and also trade liberalization within the GATT framework. The actual questionnaire, and the definitions sent with it, are reproduced as the appendix to chapter 7. A total of 40 questions were asked. It may be useful to highlight the trade scenario defined for the respondents. For bilateral free trade, firms were asked to consider the elimination of all tariff and most non-tariff barriers to trade, a dispute settlement mechanism, national treatment for investment, an end to government procurement and any other issues publicly considered to be on the table. A multilateral trade agreement was defined as that proposed at the September 1986 Uruguay GATT negotiations. In both cases it is reasonable to expect that responsible senior strategic managers would be aware of the provisions described. Thus the results of the survey can be accepted with some confidence.

The questionnaire was in two parts. The main questionnaire asked for management opinions concerning the effects of two types of trade liberalization (bilateral and multilateral) upon the operation, performance, marketing, and employment of the multinationals. Specific questions were asked about the firm's anticipated adjustment costs, need for a phase-in period, ability to substitute exporting from Canada for foreign direct investment, and attitude towards the trade negotiations.

The supplementary questionnaire focused upon bilateral trade liberalization and was of two parts. The first eleven questions were based on the strategic management model of Michael Porter (1980, 1985). Questions 1 to 5 asked how the type of competitive strategy used by the firm would be affected by a comprehensive bilateral trade agreement. Questions 6 to 8 asked how the firm would change its own strategy after such trade liberalization. In addition a question concerning world product mandates was included. Finally, two questions dealing with Porter's entry and exit barriers were included. The second part of the supplementary questionnaire asked the senior managers to forecast how key aspects of company performance would be affected by a bilateral trade agreement. Included were several questions dealing with the trade and investment decisions of the multinationals.

Before examining in detail the results of this new questionnaire a summary of the major findings on adjustment issues is given in the next section.

SUMMARY RESULTS OF SURVEY

The questionnaire was distributed in late February 1987 and responses were requested by 15 March 1987. Firms that did not respond by then were contacted and asked to reply by 30 April. The final response rate to the questionnaire was 16 out of 21 (76 percent) for Canadian-owned multinationals and 10 of 17 (59 percent) for U.S. subsidiaries in Canada. Several firms indicated that this was one of many questionnaires on free trade received over the last year. Others indicated that their responses were contingent upon the specific nature of trade liberalization and that it was difficult to make responses until the shape of the bilateral trade agreement was known.

The results are summarized in tables 7.1 to 7.4. The interpretation of these is fairly obvious and a detailed review is left to the reader. It is worth remarking that these responses confirm all of the theoretical propositions advanced earlier in this study.

On the critical questions dealing with adjustment to bilateral trade liberalization the responses of both Canadian multinationals and U.S. subsidiaries in Canada were instructive. It will be noted, for example, that questions 7 and 13 are essentially sequentially related. To question 7 most of the U.S. subsidiaries reported that they would experience relatively minor adjustment costs and in question 13 they reported that they could absorb such adjustment costs. The Canadian multinationals, on average, anticipate even fewer adjustment costs and again report that they can handle them. Consistent with this are the responses to question 11; neither U.S. subsidiaries nor Canadian multinationals state that a phase-in period of 5 years is required to adjust to bilateral free trade. In terms of question 12 both U.S. subsidiaries and the Canadian multinationals feel strongly that no major adjustment assistance is required.

The executives responding to the questionnaire also throw light on the issue of whether trade and direct investment are substitutes or complements. Both sets of multinationals disagree (to virtually the same extent) with question 17, which asks if exporting will be substituted for foreign direct investment after bilateral trade liberalization. Related to this is the strong indication, from question 18, that neither of the two groups of multinationals will close down plants in Canada due to a comprehensive free-trade agreement.

DETAILED SURVEY RESULTS

The key questions are now examined in more detail. The results are presented in the diagrams reporting the percentage response rates for each of the opinions on the question. These diagrams appear at the end of the chapter.

Trade and Adjustment

From question 1 it can be seen that 75 percent of the Canadian multinationals responding believe that a CAFTA would be of benefit to their firm, while only 19 percent express mild disagreement, and the rest are neutral. All the U.S. subsidiaries indicate that a CAFTA would be of benefit to their company. The results are fairly similar for an MTA, with the Canadian firms indicating that it would be slightly more beneficial to them than a CAFTA, while the U.S. firms are more neutral to the benefits under an MTA than a CAFTA. From question 3, 90 percent of U.S. firms state that the status quo does not benefit them. Canadian firms are slightly more neutral than the U.S. firms in stating that the status quo in U.S.-Canadian relations does not benefit their company.

From question 7, 60 percent of U.S. subsidiaries indicate that they will face adjustment costs with a CAFTA, as do, approximately, 31 percent of the Canadian multinationals. Nearly 69 percent of the Canadian firms are either neutral to the subject or do not expect such costs. The results are not different for an MTA for either the U.S. firms or the Canadian firms. However some of the Canadian firms indicate that the adjustment costs under an MTA would be smaller. In question 13, both the Canadian and U.S. firms indicate (80 percent of the Canadian firms and 90 percent of the U.S. firms) that their company could absorb the adjustment costs of a CAFTA. However, in question 11, the U.S. subsidiaries are more in need of a phase-in period of at least five years. While 50 percent of the U.S. firms indicated such a need, 62 percent of the Canadian firms rejected the idea. In a similar vein, in question 12 both sets of multinationals state strongly that they would not need adjustment assistance to survive with a CAFTA.

Question 18 indicates that 75 percent of the Canadian multinationals disagree with the statement that their company would close down plants in Canada due to a CAFTA. Similarly 70 percent of the U.S. firms disavowed such an intention. On average only 12 percent indicate that they would close down plants. Several U.S. subsidiaries indicate (in attached comments) that they would indeed close down some plants but that others would be opened in their place. They also state that plant closures and openings are a normal part of their operations over time.

According to question 9, 68 percent of Canadian multinationals and 70 percent of U.S. subsidiaries state that their workers would benefit from a CAFTA. An average 12 percent of U.S. subsidiaries and Canadian MNEs express mild disagreement with this. The results are similar for an MTA, although the U.S. subsidiaries are slightly more neutral or reserved as to whether their workers would benefit or not. On the related question of whether employment in their company would increase or decrease, 80 percent of the U.S. firms indicate that their employment would grow or at least remain the same. In supplementary question 13, only 10 percent indicate that there would be a decline in employment. The majority of Canadian firms (60 percent) indicate that they expect their employment levels to remain the same, and about 19 percent of the firms expect an increase of up to 10 percent in employment growth. Only 6 percent of the Canadian multinationals and 10 percent of the U.S. firms expect a decline of up to 10 percent in their employment levels.

Investment and Trade

According to supplementary question 19, 50 percent of the Canadian multinationals expect their investment in Canada to grow between 10 and 20 percent after a CAFTA has been in place for five years. Just over 30 percent expect their level of investment to remain the same. No firms expect a decline in investment while just over 18 percent did not answer the question. The results are similar for the U.S. subsidiaries, with 70 percent indicating an expected growth of between 10 and 20 percent. Thirty percent indicate that investment levels would stay the same after five years.

Supplementary question 18, indicates that 50 percent of Canadian firms do not expect FDI by their company to grow or decline. However, four times as many firms expect an increase in FDI of between 10 and 20 percent than expect a decline. The majority (70 percent) of U.S. subsidiaries also do not expect any change in the level of FDI by their company. From question 17 it appears that exporting is complementary to FDI for most of the firms. None of the U.S. and Canadian firms indicate that they would give up exporting for FDI. Over 55 percent of the Canadian firms and 30 percent of the U.S. firms express disagreement that they would substitute exporting for FDI; the remaining firms are neutral in their opinion.

A related question, 16, indicates that most of the Canadian firms (50 percent) believe that, after a CAFTA, they would benefit from national treatment for direct investment. However, 19 percent of the Canadian firms and only 10 percent of the U.S. subsidiaries indicated that national treatment would not benefit their firm.

Trade Effects of Trade Liberalization

The response by the members of the billion dollar club to questions on the trade-related aspects of trade liberalization are also instructive. The effects of a CAFTA after five years would result in an increase in exports, imports, and intra-firm trade for the U.S. subsidiaries and the Canadian multinationals.

According to supplementary questions 15 and 16, over 56 percent of the Canadian multinationals indicate that their exports would grow between 10 and 20 percent. While 25 percent of these firms do not expect any change in exports, twice as many do not expect imports to rise or fall. Also from questions 15 and 16 it is apparent that 90 percent of the U.S. firms indicate that their exports would increase between 10 and 20 percent. Seventy percent of the U.S. subsidiaries also indicate that their imports would rise, but not by as much as their exports. According to supplementary question 17 most of the U.S. subsidiaries (60 percent) feel that their intra-firm sales would increase by 10 to 20 percent after a CAFTA. A similar percentage of the Canadian firms indicate that their intra-firm sales would not change.

Since exporting, importing, and FDI are affected by the exchange rate, question 14 of the questionnaire asked whether it would be necessary to have a devalued exchange rate after a CAFTA for the firms to carry on exporting. Ninety percent of the U.S. subsidiaries (and 50 percent of the Canadian firms) state that they need not have a devalued Canadian dollar to be successful at exporting. Twenty-five percent of the Canadian firms are neutral to the question, with just over 12 percent being in favour of a devalued exchange rate. One firm indicates in supplementary correspondence that its analysis was dependent on knowledge of a specific exchange rate.

Performance of Multinationals
After Trade Liberalization

According to supplementary question 1, under a CAFTA the majority of Canadian multinationals believe that they will retain their competitive edge. Seventy-five percent of these firms strongly disagree with the idea that a CAFTA would benefit existing worldwide competitors at the expense of their company. In supplementary question 3, over 60 percent agree that a CAFTA would not benefit producers of substitutes for their products or services. Moreover in supplementary question 2, over 60 percent of the Canadian multinationals either agree or are neutral to the idea that a CAFTA would benefit potential entrants to their industry.

Also from supplementary questions 1 and 2, the U.S. subsidiaries agree that their international competitive position would not be eroded after a CAFTA. Eighty percent of them indicate that a CAFTA would not benefit existing worldwide competitors at the expense of the company. Fewer U.S. firms (40 percent) than Canadian firms agree that a CAFTA would not benefit producers of substitutes for their products or services. However, more U.S. firms (40 percent) than Canadian (25 percent) firms believe that a CAFTA would benefit potential entrants to their industry. In fact 80 percent of all U.S. firms either agree or remain neutral to the proposition.

Sixty-two percent of Canadian multinationals do not expect the bargaining power of suppliers to their company to increase under a CAFTA. Similarly 70 percent of the U.S. subsidiaries also agree. Forty percent of U.S. subsidiaries mildly agree that a CAFTA would increase the bargaining power of buyers of their goods and services. Canadian multinationals, however, disagree more firmly than the U.S. subsidiaries that a CAFTA would increase their buyers bargaining power, with over 30 percent strongly disagreeing, 25 percent mildly disagreeing and 25 percent remaining neutral on the issue. Only a little more than 12 percent mildly agree that their buyers bargaining power would increase with a CAFTA.

An important consideration of a CAFTA is the effect it will have on the firms' bottom line. This is dependent on the ability of a company to market and sell its products successfully. According to question 15 the majority of Canadian multinationals are neutral as to whether or not after a CAFTA their firms would find marketing easier. However, a little more than 18 percent strongly agree that they would find marketing easier, while 25 percent mildly agree. Just over 6 percent strongly disagree, with the same number not answering the question. The results were very similar for the U.S. subsidiaries, with 80 percent agreeing that marketing would be easier after a CAFTA.

Accordingly, both the U.S. and Canadian firms expect their sales to rise. From supplementary question 12 it can be seen that 80 percent of the U.S. firms expect them to rise by 10 to 20 percent, while a little over 56 percent of Canadian firms expect similar increases. Twenty percent of U.S. firms, and 25 percent of the Canadian, do not expect any change in the level of their sales due to a CAFTA.

No Canadian multinational or U.S. subsidiary according to supplementary question 20 expects a decline in profits after a CAFTA. Over 56 percent of Canadian firms expect their profits to rise between 10 and 20 percent. Twenty-five percent did not answer the question, while a little over 18 percent expect no change in profits after five years with a CAFTA. The U.S. subsidiaries were split equally between zero, 10, and 20 percent growth in profits, with 30 percent in each category. Ten percent of these firms did not answer the question.

After a CAFTA, the majority of U.S. and Canadian firms expect that they will be paying more taxes. Nearly 60 percent of the Canadian multinationals according to question

14 expect to be paying at least 10 percent more in taxes, while 25 percent expect to be paying the same amount. A little over 18 percent did not answer the question. Fifty percent of the U.S. subsidiaries indicate that they would be paying 10 percent more in taxes, while 20 percent expect to be paying up to 20 percent more in taxes after five years with a CAFTA. Thirty percent expect to be paying the same amount.

Competitive Strategies and Trade Liberalization

The Canadian multinationals and U.S. subsidiaries indicate that they would continue their strategies of cost competitiveness, product differentiation, and focus (finding niches) after a CAFTA. Approximately 70 percent of the Canadian multinationals strongly agree that they would follow the strategies of product differentiation and niching, while nearly 63 percent indicate that they strongly agree they would follow a cost competitive strategy. The results are similar for the U.S. subsidiaries in Canada. Ninety percent of the U.S. firms agree that they would follow a cost competitive strategy (60 percent very strongly), while 70 percent of the firms indicated they would continue to follow a product differentiation strategy and 80 percent agree they would follow a niching or focus strategy. The high percentages recorded for each strategy is probably determined by the diversified structures of these MNEs. Each firm probably uses different strategies in different units of the firm.

Most Canadian multinationals (44 percent) are neutral to the question of whether their ability to develop new world product mandates will be helped by a CAFTA. Thirty percent of the U.S. subsidiaries are neutral to an increase in world product mandating, however 50 percent agree that new world product mandates would be developed under a CAFTA. The more positive response by U.S. firms is probably accounted for by their nature as foreign subsidiaries. Presumably, the Canadian firms already have more activity at their Canadian home bases.

The majority, or nearly 63 percent of Canadian multinationals do not appear to believe that entry barriers will make rival firms better able to compete after a CAFTA. See supplementary question 10. Sixty percent of the U.S. subsidiaries also agree that a CAFTA would not make it more difficult for rival firms to compete due to their use of entry barriers. However, nearly twice as many U.S. subsidiaries (30 percent) as Canadian firms are neutral on this question.

On the issue of whether exit barriers will preclude their company from closing plants in Canada after a CAFTA, according to supplementary question 22, 40 percent of the U.S. subsidiaries mildly agree, 20 percent are neutral, while 40 percent disagree (30 percent very strongly). The majority or 50 percent of Canadian multinationals disagree (nearly 19 percent very strongly) with the question. Nearly 13 percent are neutral, while just over 18 percent agree. Another 18 percent of the Canadian firms did not answer the question.

CONCLUSIONS

The major themes of this study have been that multinational enterprises are efficient organizations and that their internal markets help to bypass government-imposed barriers to trade. The largest 36 multinationals (with sales of over one billion dollars) account for a substantial proportion of bilateral trade. When trade liberalization occurs, the major burden of adjustment will fall upon these large multinational enterprises. The results of the theoretical and empirical analysis of this study, coupled with the responses by these firms to the questionnaire, indicate that there will be few adjustment costs of trade liberalization.

Perhaps the most interesting result of the questionnaire is that the responses by the U.S. subsidiaries in Canada are virtually identical to those of Canadian multinationals. Both groups are strongly in favour of trade liberalization and both state that they will be able to readily adjust to new bilateral and multilateral trade regimes. There is no evidence in these responses that U.S. subsidiaries in Canada will close plants and create job losses. Instead, they anticipate that employment will increase in their companies and that their workers will benefit from trade liberalization.

Both the Canadian multinationals and the U.S. subsidiaries in Canada report that they will be able to absorb adjustment costs, that they do not require long phase-ins, a devalued exchange rate, nor adjustment assistance. They report that they will not close down plants after trade liberalization. The strength of these responses, as illustrated in tables 7.1 to 7.4, leads to the unambiguous conclusion that the major private sector firms involved in bilateral trade and production will be able to handle the transition to a free trade environment.

Not surprisingly these large companies also endorse the federal government's approach to bilateral negotiations and believe that the provincial governments should support the federal approach. They also believe that both bilateral and multilateral trade agreements will be of benefit to their companies, their workers and to Canada. They also believe that the status quo in both bilateral and multilateral trade relations is harmful to themselves.

The supplementary questionnaire was designed to explore in more detail the responses of the two sets of multinationals to a bilateral trade agreement. The responses to the questions based on the framework of Porter (1980, 1985) indicate that these companies believe that their competitive strengths will be retained after trade liberalization. The responses of the Canadian MNEs were on the whole neutral. However, both Canadian and U.S. subsidiaries view trade liberalization as likely to improve their performance. For example, 37 percent of the Canadian firms projected a 10 percent rise in sales and profits, and the next largest block saw no major change in either variable. The U.S. subsidiaries are more bullish on free trade; 30 percent expect sales to rise by 10 percent and 40 percent expect it to rise by 20 percent. Similarly 30 percent of these U.S. firms expect profit to rise by 30 percent, and 60 percent expect it to rise by over 10 percent.

It should be noted that several companies indicated that their responses to the supplementary questionnaires were contingent upon the nature of the details of a bilateral trade agreement being fully known. It was also indicated that the diverse lines of business in some of these multinationals might be affected in different ways. To investigate fully the adjustment mechanisms in these corporations it would be necessary to conduct detailed interviews. Indeed, several companies invited such interviews. In order to generate such detailed information on the adjustment mechanism within multinational enterprises, future research should use interviews to supplement the questionnaires used here.

Another implication of these findings on trade liberalization and multinational enterprises is to support the key conclusions of a recent study by Erdilek (1986). He contrasts a pessimistic argument, where a free-trade area generates "massive U.S. disinvestment and substantial Canadian de-industrialization" with an optimistic argument where such predictions are unfounded or exaggerated. (Note that he does not consider Canadian investment in the United States.) Erdilek finds conceptual and some case support for the optimistic over the pessimistic argument but concludes that even it is "mostly speculative and suggestive." As this study has demonstrated his conclusions are far too modest. In this work, theoretical, empirical, and survey analysis served to reinforce each other in predicting that large multinational enterprises could bear the burden of adjustment to trade liberalization as a normal part of their strategic management.

Table 7.1
MAIN QUESTIONNAIRE
CANADIAN MNEs RESPONSE RATES

Name of Company _____

	Strongly Agree	Strongly Disagree	Mean
1. A CAFTA will be of benefit to my company.	1 —2— 3	4 5	1.8
2. An MTA will be of benefit to my company.	1 —2— 3	4 5	1.6
3. The status quo in U.S.-Canadian trade relations benefits my company.	1 2 3	—4— 5	4.1
4. The status quo in multilateral trade relations benefits my company.	1 2 3	—4— 5	3.9
5. Canada as a whole will benefit from a CAFTA.	1 —2— 3	4 5	1.5
6. Canada as a whole will benefit from an MTA.	1 —2— 3	4 5	1.5
7. My company will experience adjustment costs with a CAFTA.	1 2 3	—4 5	3.1
8. My company will experience adjustment costs with an MTA.	1 2 3	—4 5	3.3
9. My workers will benefit from a CAFTA.	1 2— 3	4 5	2.1
10. My workers will benefit from an MTA.	1 —2— 3	4 5	1.9
11. My company needs a phase-in period of at least 5 years to adjust to a CAFTA.	1 2 3	—4 5	3.8
12. My company requires major adjustment assistance to survive with a CAFTA.	1 2 3	—4— 5	4.6
13. My company can absorb the adjustment costs of a CAFTA.	1 —2— 3	4 5	1.8
14. After a CAFTA my company will need a devalued exchange rate to be successful in exporting.	1 2 3	—4 5	3.9
15. After a CAFTA my company will find marketing easier.	1 2— 3	4 5	2.5
16. After a CAFTA my company will benefit from national treatment for direct investment.	1 2 —3	4 5	2.6
17. After a CAFTA my company will substitute exporting from Canada for foreign direct investment.	1 2 3	—4 5	3.8
18. My company will close down plants in Canada due to a CAFTA.	1 2 3	—4— 5	4.1
19. My company supports the federal government's approach to the CAFTA negotiations.	1 —2— 3	4 5	1.6
20. My company believes that the provincial governments should support the federal approach to the CAFTA negotiations.	1—2— 3	4 5	1.4

Please write any comments on the reverse side.

Table 7.2
MAIN QUESTIONNAIRE
Name of Company _____ U. S. SUBSIDIARIES RESPONSE RATES

	Strongly Agree				Strongly Disagree	Mean
1. A CAFTA will be of benefit to my company.	1	2	3	4	5	1.6
2. An MTA will be of benefit to my company.	1	2	3	4	5	2.3
3. The status quo in U.S.-Canadian trade relations benefits my company.	1	2	3	4	5	4.2
4. The status quo in multilateral trade relations benefits my company.	1	2	3	4	5	3.9
5. Canada as a whole will benefit from a CAFTA.	1	2	3	4	5	1.2
6. Canada as a whole will benefit from an MTA.	1	2	3	4	5	1.8
7. My company will experience adjustment costs with a CAFTA.	1	2	3	4	5	2.6
8. My company will experience adjustment costs with an MTA.	1	2	3	4	5	2.9
9. My workers will benefit from a CAFTA.	1	2	3	4	5	2.1
10. My workers will benefit from an MTA.	1	2	3	4	5	2.6
11. My company needs a phase-in period of at least 5 years to adjust to a CAFTA.	1	2	3	4	5	3.2
12. My company requires major adjustment assistance to survive with a CAFTA.	1	2	3	4	5	4.5
13. My company can absorb the adjustment costs of a CAFTA.	1	2	3	4	5	1.8
14. After a CAFTA my company will need a devalued exchange rate to be successful in exporting.	1	2	3	4	5	4.3
15. After a CAFTA my company will find marketing easier.	1	2	3	4	5	2.0
16. After a CAFTA my company will benefit from national treatment for direct investment.	1	2	3	4	5	2.2
17. After a CAFTA my company will substitute exporting from Canada for foreign direct investment.	1	2	3	4	5	3.8
18. My company will close down plants in Canada due to a CAFTA.	1	2	3	4	5	3.7
19. My company supports the federal government's approach to the CAFTA negotiations.	1	2	3	4	5	1.6
20. My company believes that the provincial governments should support the federal approach to the CAFTA negotiations.	1	2	3	4	5	1.4

Please write any comments on the reverse side.

Table 7.3

SUPPLEMENTARY QUESTIONNAIRE

CANADIAN MNEs RESPONSE RATES

Name of Company _____

	Strongly Agree	Strongly Disagree	Mean
1. A CAFTA will benefit existing worldwide competitors at the expense of my company.	1 2 3—4—5		4.5
2. A CAFTA will benefit potential entrants to my industry.	1 2 3—4 5		3.4
3. A CAFTA will benefit producers of substitutes for my products or services.	1 2 3—4 5		3.9
4. A CAFTA will increase the bargaining power of suppliers to my company.	1 2 3—4—5		4.1
5. A CAFTA will increase the bargaining power of buyers of my goods or services.	1 2 3—4 5		3.8
6. Our strategy of cost competition will be continued after a CAFTA.	1—2—3 4 5		1.3
7. Our strategy of product differentiation will be continued after a CAFTA.	1—2—3 4 5		1.4
8. Our strategy of focus (finding niches) will be continued after a CAFTA.	1—2—3 4 5		1.3
9. Our ability to develop new world product mandates will be helped by a CAFTA.	1 2—3 4 5		2.7
10. A CAFTA will make it more difficult for rival firms to compete with my company, due to our use of entry barriers.	1 2 3—4 5		3.9
11. Exit barriers will preclude my company from closing plants in Canada after a CAFTA.	1 2 3—4 5		3.5

	5 Year Total (Percentage)	Mean
Forecasting: After a CAFTA has been in place for 5 years the following net changes will occur:		
12. Sales of my company will decrease/increase:	−20 −10 0 10 20	9.2
13. Employment in my company will increase/decrease by:	−20 −10 0 10 20	1.5
14. Taxes paid to Canadian governments by my company will decrease/increase by:	−20 −10 0 10 20	6.9
15. Exports of my company will decrease/increase by:	−20 −10 0 10 20	9.2
16. Imports of my company will decrease/increase by:	−20 −10 0 10 20	1.5
17. Intra-firm trade of my company will decrease/increase by:	−20 −10 0 10 20	2.3
18. Foreign direct investment by my company will decrease/increase by:	−20 −10 0 10 20	3.1
19. Investment in Canada by my company will decrease/increase by:	−20 −10 0 10 20	9.2
20. Profits (return on equity) of my company will decrease/increase by:	−20 −10 0 10 20	10.0

Please write any comments on the reverse side.

Table 7.4
SUPPLEMENTARY QUESTIONNAIRE
CANADIAN MNEs RESPONSE RATES

Name of Company _____

	Strongly Agree				Strongly Disagree	Mean

1. A CAFTA will benefit existing worldwide competitors at the expense of my company. — 1 2 3 4 5 — 4.5

2. A CAFTA will benefit potential entrants to my industry. — 1 2 3 4 5 — 2.9

3. A CAFTA will benefit producers of substitutes for my products or services. — 1 2 3 4 5 — 3.6

4. A CAFTA will increase the bargaining power of suppliers to my company. — 1 2 3 4 5 — 3.8

5. A. CAFTA will increase the bargaining power of buyers of my goods or services. — 1 2 3 4 5 — 3.1

6. Our strategy of cost competition will be continued after a CAFTA. — 1 2 3 4 5 — 1.5

7. Our strategy of product differentiation will be continued after a CAFTA. — 1 2 3 4 5 — 1.8

8. Our strategy of focus (finding niches) will be continued after a CAFTA. — 1 2 3 4 5 — 1.6

9. Our ability to develop new world product mandates will be helped by a CAFTA. — 1 2 3 4 5 — 2.4

10. A CAFTA will make it more difficult for rival firms to compete with my company, due to our use of entry barriers. — 1 2 3 4 5 — 3.9

11. Exit barriers will preclude my company from closing plants in Canada after a CAFTA. — 1 2 3 4 5 — 3.3

Forecasting: After a CAFTA has been in place for 5 years the following net changes will occur: 5 Year Total (Percentage)

12. Sales of my company will decrease/increase: — -20 -10 0 10 20 — 12.0

13. Employment in my company will increase/decrease by: — -20 -10 0 10 20 — 6.7

14. Taxes paid to Canadian governments by my company will decrease/increase by: — -20 -10 0 10 20 — 9.0

15. Exports of my company will decrease/increase by: — -20 -10 0 10 20 — 14.0

16. Imports of my company will decrease/increase by: — -20 -10 0 10 20 — 10.0

17. Intra-firm trade of my company will decrease/increase by: — -20 -10 0 10 20 — 8.9

18. Foreign direct investment by my company will decrease/increase by: — -20 -10 0 10 20 — 2.5

19. Investment in Canada by my company will decrease/increase by: — -20 -10 0 10 20 — 10.0

20. Profits (return on equity) of my company will decrease/increase by: — -20 -10 0 10 20 — 10.0

Please write any comments on the reverse side.

Free Trade Questionnaire and Responses to Selected Questions

SCORING KEY: Please circle *ONLY* one opinion per question.

1 = Strongly agree
2 = Mildly agree
3 = Neither agree nor disagree
4 = Mildly disagree
5 = Strongly disagree

DEFINITIONS

CAFTA: A Canadian-American free trade area (the elimination of all tariff and non-tariff barriers to trade, including a new trade disputes settlement mechanism; national treatment for investment; termination of government procurement and other trade-related measures), as currently being negotiated by Ambassador Reisman.

MTA: A multilateral trade agreement, as proposed at the September 1986 Uruguay Round of the GATT; expected to be negotiated over the next four (4) years.

BENEFIT: Improved economic performance (however measured)

NATIONAL TREATMENT: The same treatment for foreign-owned and domestic corporations with respect to government regulations.

WORLD PRODUCT MANDATE: A charter granted by the parent firm to a subsidiary to develop, produce and market worldwide a new product line.

ENTRY BARRIERS: Any of: scale economies, product differentiation, capital requirements, switching (supplier) costs, distribution channels, government regulations.

EXIT BARRIERS: (broadly similar to above, but acting in the reverse manner).

CONFIDENTIALITY

Your replies will be treated in the strictest confidence by Professor Rugman and not released to any organization or individual. All information will be aggregated and published only in general form.

Please return (in the enclosed stamped envelope) before 15th March to:
Professor Alan M. Rugman
Centre for International Business Studies
Dalhousie University
Halifax, Nova Scotia, B3H 1Z5

163

MAIN QUESTIONAIRE

Name of Company _____

	Strongly Agree				Strongly Disagree
1. A CAFTA will be of benefit to my company.	1	2	3	4	5
2. An MTA will be of benefit to my company.	1	2	3	4	5
3. The status quo in U.S.-Canadian trade relations benefits my company.	1	2	3	4	5
4. The status quo in multilateral trade relations benefits my company.	1	2	3	4	5
5. Canada as a whole will benefit from a CAFTA.	1	2	3	4	5
6. Canada as a whole will benefit from an MTA.	1	2	3	4	5
7. My company will experience adjustment costs with a CAFTA.	1	2	3	4	5
8. My company will experience adjustment costs with an MTA.	1	2	3	4	5
9. My workers will benefit from a CAFTA.	1	2	3	4	5
10. My workers will benefit from an MTA.	1	2	3	4	5
11. My company needs a phase-in period of at least 5 years to adjust to a CAFTA.	1	2	3	4	5
12. My company requires major adjustment assistance to survive with a CAFTA.	1	2	3	4	5
13. My company can absorb the adjustment costs of a CAFTA.	1	2	3	4	5
14. After a CAFTA my company will need a devalued exchange rate to be successful in exporting.	1	2	3	4	5
15. After a CAFTA my company will find marketing easier.	1	2	3	4	5
16. After a CAFTA my company will benefit from national treatment for direct investment.	1	2	3	4	5
17. After a CAFTA my company will substitute exporting from Canada for foreign direct investment.	1	2	3	4	5
18. My company will close down plants in Canada due to a CAFTA.	1	2	3	4	5
19. My company supports the federal government's approach to the CAFTA negotiations.	1	2	3	4	5
20. My company believes that the provincial governments should support the federal approach to the CAFTA negotiations.	1	2	3	4	5

Please write any comments on the reverse side.

SUPPLEMENTARY QUESTIONAIRE

Name of Company _____

		Strongly Agree			Strongly Disagree	
1.	A CAFTA will benefit existing worldwide competitors at the expense of my company.	1	2	3	4	5
2.	A CAFTA will benefit potential entrants to my industry.	1	2	3	4	5
3.	A CAFTA will benefit producers of substitutes for my products or services.	1	2	3	4	5
4.	A CAFTA will increase the bargaining power of suppliers to my company.	1	2	3	4	5
5.	A CAFTA will increase the bargaining power of buyers of my goods or services.	1	2	3	4	5
6.	Our strategy of cost competition will be continued after a CAFTA.	1	2	3	4	5
7.	Our strategy of product differentiation will be continued after a CAFTA.	1	2	3	4	5
8.	Our strategy of focus (finding niches) will be continued after a CAFTA.	1	2	3	4	5
9.	Our ability to develop new world product mandates will be helped by a CAFTA.	1	2	3	4	5
10.	A CAFTA will make it more difficult for rival firms to compete with my company, due to our use of entry barriers.	1	2	3	4	5
11.	Exit barriers will preclude my company from closing plants in Canada after a CAFTA.	1	2	3	4	5

Forecasting: After a CAFTA has been in place for 5 years the following net changes will occur:

5 Year Total (Percentage)

12.	Sales of my company will decrease/increase:	−20	−10	0	10	20
13.	Employment in my company will increase/decrease by:	−20	−10	0	10	20
14.	Taxes paid to Canadian governments by my company will decrease/increase by:	−20	−10	0	10	20
15.	Exports of my company will decrease/increase by:	−20	−10	0	10	20
16.	Imports of my company will decrease/increase by:	−20	−10	0	10	20
17.	Intra-firm trade of my company will decrease/increase by:	−20	−10	0	10	20
18.	Foreign direct investment by my company will decrease/increase by:	−20	−10	0	10	20
19.	Investment in Canada by my company will decrease/increase by:	−20	−10	0	10	20
20.	Profits (return on equity) of my company will decrease/increase by:	−20	−10	0	10	20

Please write any comments on the reverse side.

Question 1
A CAFTA will be of benefit to my company.

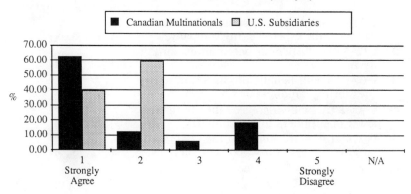

Question 3
The status quo in U.S.-Canada trade relations benefits my company.

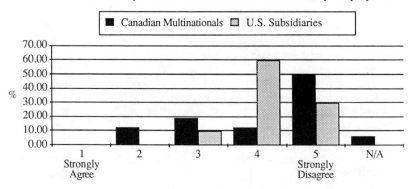

Question 7
My company will experience adjustment costs with a CAFTA.

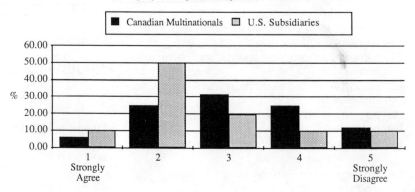

Question 9
My workers will benefit from a CAFTA.

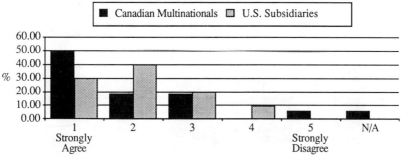

Question 11
My company needs a phase-in period
of at least 5 years to adjust to a CAFTA

App B

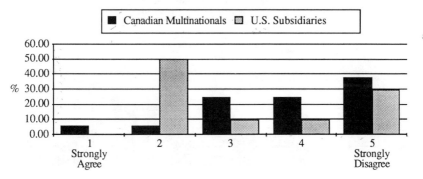

Question 12
My company requires major adjustment
assistance to survive with a CAFTA.

App C

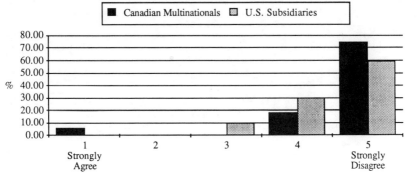

Question 13
My company can absorb the adjustment costs of a CAFTA.

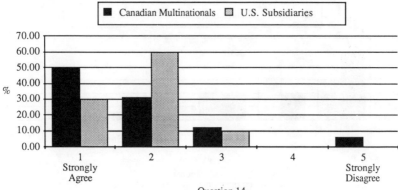

Question 14
After a CAFTA my company will
need a devalued exchange rate to be
successful in exporting.

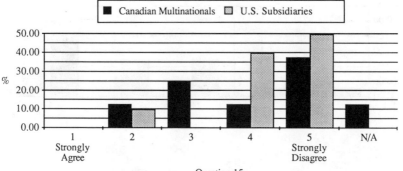

Question 15
After a CAFTA my company will find marketing easier.

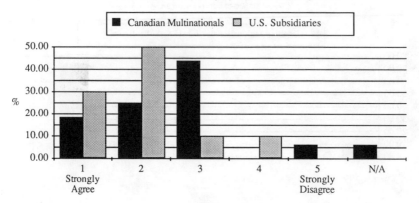

Responses to Selected Questions

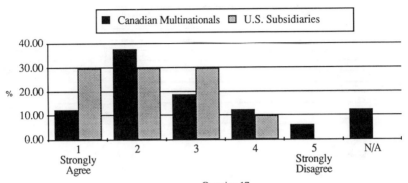

Question 16
After a CAFTA my company will benefit from
national treatment for direct investment.

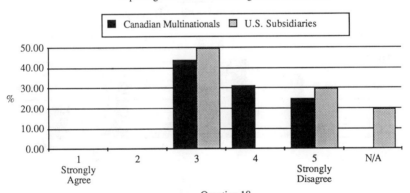

Question 17
After a CAFTA my company will substitute
exporting from Canada for foreign direct investment.

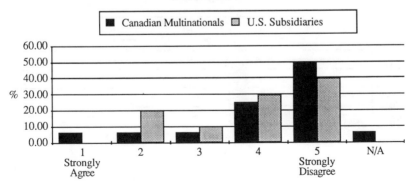

Question 18
My company will close down plants
in Canada due to a CAFTA.

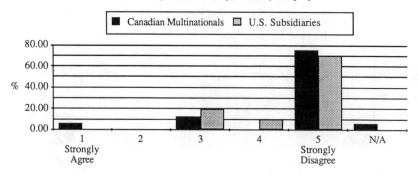

Supplementary Question 1
A CAFTA will benefit existing worldwide
competitors at the expense of my company.

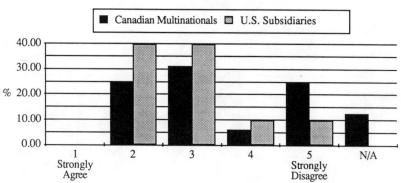

Supplementary Question 2
A CAFTA will benefit potential entrants to my industry.

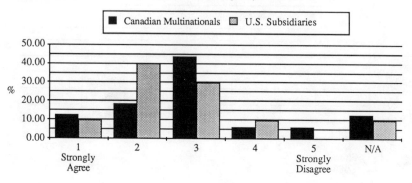

Supplementary Question 9
Our ability to develop new world product
mandates will be helped by a CAFTA.

Supplementary Question 10
A CAFTA will make it more difficult for
rival firms to compete with my company
due to our use of entry barriers.

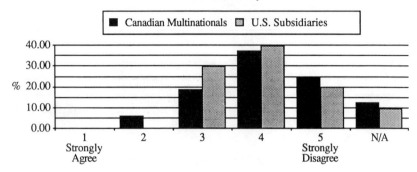

Supplementary Question 11
Exit barriers will preclude my company from
closing plants in Canada after a CAFTA.

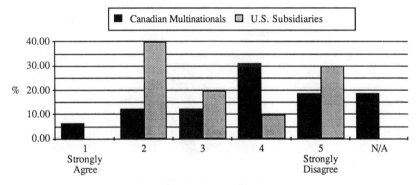

Supplementary Question 12
Sales of my company will decrease/increase by:

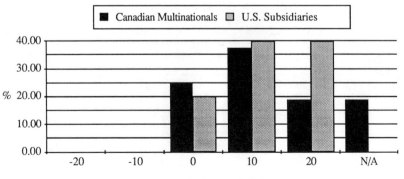

Supplementary Question 13
Employment in my company will decrease/increase by:

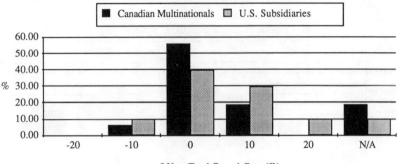

5 Year Total Growth Rate (%)

Supplementary Question 14
Taxes paid to Canadian governments
by my company will decrease/increase by:

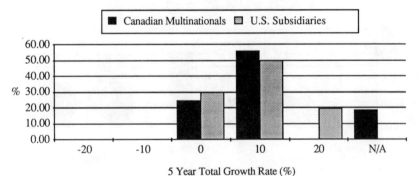

5 Year Total Growth Rate (%)

Supplementary Question 15
Exports of my company will decrease/increase by:

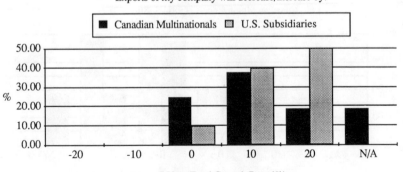

5 Year Total Growth Rate (%)

Supplementary Question 16
Imports of my company will decrease/increase by:

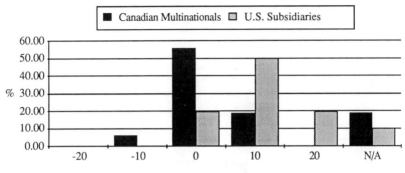

Supplementary Question 17
Intra-firm trade of my company will decrease/increase by:

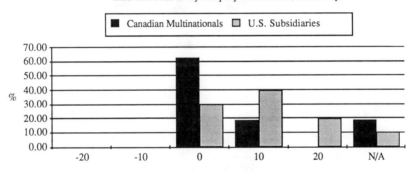

Supplementary Question 18
Foreign direct investment by my company
will decrease/increase by:

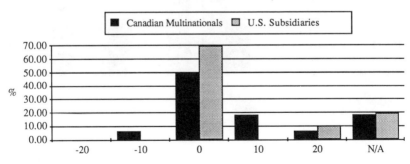

Supplementary Question 19
Investment in Canada by my company will
decrease/increase by:

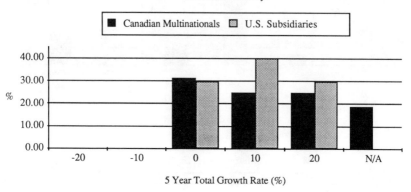

5 Year Total Growth Rate (%)

Supplementary Question 20
Profits (return on equity) of my company will decrease/increase by:

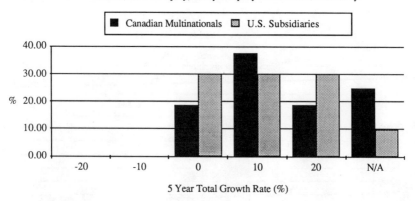

5 Year Total Growth Rate (%)

Chapter 8

Conclusions and Policy Implications

The major findings of this study are built upon both theoretical and empirical research. At the theoretical level the existing literature on the relationship between trade and investment was reviewed and synthesized in chapters 2 and 6 to demonstrate that trade and direct investment are complements rather than substitutes. This finding is based on a management assessment of environmental factors influencing the decision to service foreign markets. When there is an increase in U.S. non-tariff barriers to trade (for example, in the form of administered protection) Canadian firms will engage in foreign direct investment in the United States in order to retain the market access denied to exports. However, such direct investment will, in time, generate exports from the parent (Canadian) firm to its (U.S.) subsidiary, thereby leading to a complementary increase in trade along with investment.

Empirical work (in chapters 3 and 4) confirms that Canadian parent multinationals have large exports to their subsidiaries (the parents export five times as much as they import from their U.S. subsidiaries). The trade surplus by Canada's multinationals is, of course, partly offset by the purchases of U.S. subsidiaries in Canada from their American parents. However, it is demonstrated that since 1975 there have been greater net outflows than inflows of direct investment into Canada, such that today, the Canadian stock of direct investment in the United States is about 60 percent of the American stock in Canada. Thus, one of the key contributions of this study is to emphasize the emergence of Canadian-owned multinationals in the United States and the opportunities available to them in a new trading environment.

The empirical work in this book on the activities of Canadian-owned multinationals operating in the United

States is entirely new. It provides valuable insights into the nature of an activity that has been largely neglected in research and public policy analysis. The new work was balanced by an updated study of the performance of foreign-owned firms in Canada. An important finding in chapter 3 is that U.S. subsidiaries in Canada export, on average, about 25 percent of their output, so that they can hardly be classified as being in Canada entirely for reasons of import substitution. This, and related findings, calls into question the old fashioned view of foreign subsidiaries as being purely tariff factories. This evidence also questions the "deindustrialization" thesis when it is demonstrated that the extent of foreign ownership is declining and is now matched by an equivalent amount of Canadian-owned outward direct investment. The "reindustrialization" of Canada is embodied in Canada's new and successful multinationals identified in chapter 5.

These data on the trade performance of multinationals confirm the basic premise of this study, namely that there is a large amount of bilateral intra-industry trade. The data compiled and analyzed in this study (at aggregate level in chapters 3 and 4 and at firm level in chapter 5) confirm previous studies of intra-industry trade by MacCharles (1985b, 1987) and others. All the evidence points toward a high degree of integration of the U.S. and Canadian economies, fostered by the operations of multinational enterprises. For example, one aspect of this research was empirical work in chapters 3 and 4 on the nature of intra-industry trade by all the multinational enterprises involved in the Canadian economy. Also reported was the extent of intra-industry production reported in chapter 4. A variant of this is the index of the national balance of production which is calculated as 0.74 for 1982. This is comparable to figures by EEC nations and is significantly higher than Japan's index of 0.38. The index for the national balance of production attests to the high degree of bilateral economic integration. This interaction is, in turn, basically dependent upon the production and trade by the largest multinationals, which are vehicles for North American economic interdependence.

Building on the large multinationals identified in chapter 5 with net sales of one billion dollars or more, chapter 6 developed conceptual answers to how these firms would adjust to trade liberalization. This detailed and technical investigation of the competitive strategies of these multinational enterprises, based upon the model of Porter (1980, 1985), suggested that their strategic planners are well equipped to pilot their firms through the shocks of new trading regimes. It was found that most operations of Canadian and U.S. multinationals in Canada are characterized by strong firm specific advantages. Their competitive strengths are not dependent upon trade barriers so that structural adjustments after bilateral trade liberalization will be minimal.

The theoretical implications were fully supported in chapter 7 by the results of a survey of the chief executive officers of the largest Canadian-owned multinational enterprises in the United States and the largest U.S. subsidiaries operating in Canada. These influential executives believe that their companies can adjust efficiently to new trading regimes and that there are neutral effects on employment in the short run and beneficial effects in the long run. The key multinationals will thereby help to execute a bilateral trade agreement and minimize the adjustment costs.

The policy implications of this research are of three kinds.

First, it is necessary to recognize the vital role played by the largest multinational enterprises in bilateral trade and investment. It is necessary to involve the senior managers of these firms in the discussions of any new bilateral trading regime, since they control key aspects of the adjustment process.

Second, the role of branch plants in Canada should be understood from the background of management theory. There are exit barriers in the form of sunk costs that will minimize the sudden departure of foreign-owned firms originally attracted here to avoid Canadian tariffs. Moreover, most of these branch plants have access to the firm specific advantages of their parents, such as proprietary production and marketing skills; hence they will not lose their competitive advantages after trade liberalization. With trade liberalization the strategic reasons for producing in Canada will be reassessed against the new information available on glo-

bal production and marketing opportunities. In today's
competitive system, Canada will retain and attract foreign
direct investment if there is a good business climate; but
not if there are perceptions of arbitrary government regulations, taxes, tariffs, or a lack of national treatment for
investment.

Third, the opportunities for Canada's multinationals to
expand in the United States will grow with or without trade
liberalization. In either case, Canada's primary market in
the United States can be secured by Canadian firms. With
free trade Canada can have more domestic production and
exports. Without it, Canada will have more direct investment and foreign production. However, this will still contribute to Canada's wealth since Canada's subsidiaries in
the United States will purchase a proportion of their supplies and components from their parent Canadian firm.
Also dividends will be remitted to Canada thereby increasing its national income and potential for job creation.

In conclusion, it is apparent that analysis of the adjustment costs of trade liberalization needs to incorporate
managerial factors, especially the role of multinational
enterprises. The large amount of intra-industry trade and
investment by both U.S. and Canadian-owned multinationals serves to strengthen the economic integration of
North America. Due to such integration the prospect of bilateral trade liberalization is not as disruptive as purely
economics-based models might suggest. Multinational enterprises are the solution, rather than a problem, in the
process of implementation of the Canada-U.S. free trade
agreement.

The single most important finding of this study (from
chapter 7) is that trade liberalization will be welcomed by
multinational enterprises. It will not lead to major (or even
minor) adjustment costs in Canada since most multinational enterprises are now well positioned to absorb such
environmental changes. Due to the efficient nature of their
systems of internal strategic planning neither U.S. subsidiaries in Canada nor Canadian multinationals operating in
the United States will experience plant closures or worker
layoffs.

The theoretical, empirical, and survey results all demonstrate that trade liberalization will present opportunities for the further economic integration of the United States and Canada, leading to increases in employment and output by both sets of multinational enterprises. Indeed, the favourable economic climate following trade liberalization will probably lead to greater inflows of direct investment into Canada from third countries, including Japan and European nations. The overall stimulation of direct investment in North America after bilateral trade liberalization will be of undoubted benefit to the citizens of Canada and the United States.

References

Aho, C. Michael, and Marc Levinson. "A Canadian Opportunity." *Foreign Policy* 66 (Spring 1987): 143–55.

Aquino, A. "Intra-Industry Trade and Inter-Industry Specialization as Concurrent Sources of International Trade in Manufactures." *Weltwirtschaftliches Archiv Bd.* 114 (1978): 90–99.

Arrow, Kenneth. *Essays in the Theory of Risk-Bearing* (Chicago: Markham, 1971).

Balassa, Bela. "Intra-Industry Specialization: A Cross-Country Analysis." *European Economic Review* 30 (1986): 27–42.

Balcome, David. *Choosing Their Own Paths: Profiles of the Export Strategies of Canadian Manufacturers* (Ottawa: Conference Board of Canada, 1986).

Baldwin, John R. and Paul K. Gorecki. "The Relationship Between Trade and Tariff Patterns and the Efficiency of Canadian Manufacturing Sector in the 1970s: A Summary," in John Whalley and Roderick Hill, eds., *Canada-United States Free Trade*, vol. 11 (Toronto: University of Toronto Press, 1985): 179–92.

Baranson, Jack. "Assessment of Likely Impact of a U.S.-Canadian Free Trade Agreement upon the Behavior of U.S. Industrial Subsidiaries in Canada (Ontario)" (Toronto: Government of Ontario Ministry of Industry, Trade and Technology, Nov. 1985).

Bishop, Paul M., and Harold Crookell. *Specialization and Foreign Investment in Canada*. Research Study under contract to the Department of Finance, Government of Canada, School of Business Administration, University of Western Ontario, 1983.

Buckley, Peter J., and Mark Casson. *The Future of the Multinational Enterprise* (Basingstoke and London: Macmillan, 1976).

Burgess, David F. "The Impact of Trade Liberalization on Foreign Direct Investment Flows," in John Whalley and Roderick Hill, eds., *Canada-United States Free Trade*, vol. 11 (Toronto: University of Toronto Press, 1985): 193–99.

——— . "Implications of a U.S.-Canadian Trade Agreement for Factor Flows and Plant Location" (mimeo, 1986).

Canada. Department of External Affairs. "Effect of Enhanced Trade on Investment Survey Evidence" (Ottawa: 1985a).

——— . "Impact of Trade Liberalization on Investment: The Adjustment Process" (Ottawa: 1985b).

Canada. Department of Industry, Trade and Commerce. *Foreign-Owned Subsidiaries in Canada: 1964–1967* (Ottawa: Queen's Printer for Canada, 1970).

——— . *Statistical Supplement to Foreign-Owned Subsidiaries in Canada: 1964–1969* (Ottawa: Department of IT & C, Aug. 1972).

——— . *Foreign-Owned Subsidiaries in Canada: 1964–1971* (Ottawa: Information Canada, 1974).

——— . *Statistical Supplements to Foreign-Owned Subsidiaries in Canada: 1964–1971* (Ottawa: Surveys and Analysis, Statistical and Data Base Services, IT & C, May 7, 1985).

Canada. Department of Industry, Trade and Commerce/Regional Economic Expansion. *Foreign-Owned Subsidiaries in Canada: 1973–1979* (Ottawa: Surveys and Analysis, Statistical and Data Base Services, IT & C, and DRIE, Apr. 1983).

Canada. Department of Regional Industrial Expansion. *Foreign-Owned Subsidiaries in Canada: 1979–81* (Ottawa: Surveys and Analysis, Statistical and Data Base Services, DRIE, Sept. 1984).

Canada. Foreign Investment Review Agency, Policy Research Division. *Compendium of Statistics on Foreign Investment*, FIRA paper no. 4 (Ottawa: Research and Analysis Branch, May 1978).

Canada. *Royal Commission on the Economic Union and Development Prospects for Canada*, 3 vols., Donald S. Macdonald, chairman (Ottawa: Supply and Services Canada, 1985).

Canada. Statistics Canada. *Quarterly Estimates of the Canadian Balance of International Payments* (Ottawa: Supply and Services Canada, catalogue no. 67–001 quarterly, various years).

——— . *Corporations and Labour Unions Returns Act; Part 1— Corporations* (Ottawa: Supply and Services Canada, catalogue no. 61–210 annual, various years).

——— . *Domestic and Foreign Control of Manufacturing Establishments in Canada; 1972* (Ottawa: IT & C, catalogue no. 31–401, Nov. 1977).

——— . *Structural Aspects of Domestic and Foreign Control in the Manufacturing, Mining and Forestry Industries: 1970–1972*

(Ottawa: Supply and Services Canada, catalogue no. 31–523 occasional, Feb. 1978).

——— . *Domestic and Foreign Control of Manufacturing, Mining and Logging Establishments in Canada: 1981, 1976, and 1974* (Ottawa: Supply and Services Canada, catalogue no. 31–401, July 1985, Feb. 1981 and Jan. 1979).

——— . *Canadian Imports by Domestic and Foreign Controlled Enterprises: 1978* (Ottawa: Supply and Services Canada, catalogue no. 67–509 occasional, Oct. 1981).

——— . *Canadian Imports by Domestic and Foreign Controlled Enterprises: 1980* (Ottawa: Supply and Services Canada, catalogue no. 67–509 occasional, May 1985).

——— . *Canada's International Investment Position: 1981 to 1984* (Ottawa: Supply and Services Canada, catalogue no. 67–202, May 1986).

"Canada's Leading R & D Spenders." *The Financial Post* (Section 4, Oct. 25, 1986): 37.

"Canada's Top 500." *Canadian Business* (Special 1986 Annual) plus various issues.

Cantwell, John A. "Technological Competition and Intra-Industry Production in Europe." Working Paper, Presented to the European International Business Association, Department of Economics, University of Reading, Nov. 1986.

——— . *Technological Innovation and Multinational Corporations* (Oxford: Basil Blackwell, 1987), forthcoming.

Casson, Mark C. *Multinationals and World Trade* (London: Allen and Unwin, 1986).

Caves, Richard E. *Multinational Enterprise and Economic Analysis* (New York: Cambridge University Press, 1982).

Caves, Richard E., Michael E. Porter, A. Michael Spence, and John T. Scott. *Competition in the Open Economy: A Model Applied to Canada* (Cambridge, Mass.: Harvard University Press, 1980).

Chisholm, Derek. "Investment Responses by Multinational Enterprises to Three Canadian Policy Options for Canada-United States Trade" (Ottawa: The Institute for Research on Public Policy, 1985).

Coase, Ronald H. "The Nature of the Firm." *Economica* 4 (1937): 385–405.

Coopers and Lybrand Consulting Group. "Free-Trade Survey" (Feb. 1987).

Crookell, Harold, and John Caliendo. "International Competitiveness and the Structure of Secondary Industry in Canada."
Business Quarterly 45:3 (Autumn 1980): 58–64.

D'Cruz, Joseph R. "Strategic Planning in Multinational Subsidiaries." Unpublished, Working Paper no. 6, Faculty of Management
Studies, University of Toronto, 1983.

————. "Strategic Management of Subsidiaries," in Hamid Etemad and Louise Seguin Dulude, eds., *Managing the Multinational
Subsidiary* (London: Croom-Helm, 1986): 75–89.

Daly, Donald J., and Donald C. MacCharles. *Canadian Manufactured Exports: Constraints and Opportunities* (Toronto: York University, mimeo, 1983).

Doz, Yves L., and C. K. Prahalad. "Headquarters Influence and
Strategic Control in MNCs." *Sloan Management Review*, 22:1 (Fall
1981): 15–29.

Dunning, John H. *International Production and the Multinational Enterprise* (London: Allen and Unwin, 1981).

————. "A note on intra-industry foreign direct investment."
Banca Nazionale del Lavoro Quarterly Review 139 (Dec. 1980).

Dunning, John H., and Alan M. Rugman. "The Contribution of
Hymer's Dissertation to the Theory of Foreign Direct Investment."
American Economic Review 75:2 (May 1985).

Erdilek, Asim, ed. *Multinationals as Mutual Invaders: Intra-
Industry Direct Foreign Investment* (London: Croom Helm, 1985).

Erdilek, Asim. "Potential Impact of a Bilateral Free(r) Trade
Agreement on U.S. Direct Investment In Canadian Manufacturing."
Case Western Reserve University, Research Program in Industrial
Economics, Working Paper 5 (1986), Cleveland, Ohio.

Forget, Claude E., and Daniel Denis. *Canadian Foreign Direct
Investment in the United States: Reasons and Consequences*
(Montreal: C. D. Howe Institute for Policy Sector Branch, DRIE,
June 1985).

Franko, Lawrence. "European Multinational Enterprises in the
Integration Process," in Curzon and Curzon, eds., *Multinationals
in a Hostile World* (London: Macmillan, 1977).

Gandhi, Prem. "Foreign Direct Investment and Regional Devel-
opment: The Case of Canadian Investment in New York State."
Mimeo, Center for Business and Economics, State University of
New York, Plattsburgh, 1984.

Giersch, Herbert, ed. *On the Economics of Intra-Industry Trade* (Kiel University: Institute fur Weltwirtschaft; J. C. B. Mohr, 1979).

Globerman, Steven. "Direct Investment, Economic Structure, and Industrial Competitiveness: The Canadian Case," in John H. Dunning, ed., *Multinational Enterprises, Economic Structure and Industrial Competitiveness* (London: John Wiley and Sons, 1985).

Granatestein, J. L. "The Issue That Will Not Go Away: Free Trade Between Canada and the United States," in Denis Stairs and Gilbert Windham, eds., *The Politics of Canada's Economic Relationship With The United States* (Toronto: University of Toronto Press, 1985).

Greenway, D., and P. K. M. Tharakan, eds. *Imperfect Competition and International Trade: The Policy Aspects of Intra-Industry Trade* (Brighton: Wheatsheaf, 1986).

Group of Thirty. *Foreign Direct Investment 1973–1987* (New York: 1984).

Grubel, Herbert, G., and Peter J. Lloyd. *Intra-Industry Trade: The Theory of Measurement of International Trade in Differentiated Products* (London: Macmillan, 1975).

Guthrie, A. "A Brief History of Canadian-American Reciprocity," in Sperry Lea, ed., *A Canada-U.S. Free Trade Arrangement: A Survey Of Possible Characteristics* (Toronto: Canadian-American Committee, 1963).

Harris, Richard E. "Jobs and Free Trade," in David W. Conklin and Thomas J. Courchene, eds., *Canadian Trade at a Crossroads: Options for New International Agreements* (Toronto: Ontario Economic Council, 1985): 188–203.

Harris, Richard E., and D. Cox. *Trade, Industrial Policy and Canadian Manufacturing* (Ontario: Ontario Economic Council Research Study, 1983).

Helleiner, Gerald K. *Intra-Firm Trade and the Developing Countries* (London: Macmillan, 1981).

Helpman, E., and Paul R. Krugman. *Market Structure and Foreign Trade: Increasing Returns, Imperfect Competition and the International Economy* (Brighton: Wheatsheaf, 1985).

Hufbauer, Gary C., and Jeffrey J. Schott. "The Role of Bilateral Investment Talks," in David W. Conklin and Thomas J. Courchene, eds., *Canadian Trade at a Crossroads: Options for New International Agreements* (Toronto: Ontario Economic Council, 1985): 343–49.

Hymer, Stephen H. *The International Operations of National Firms: A Study of Direct Foreign Investment* (Cambridge, Mass.: MIT Press, 1976).

"Industry's 500." *The Financial Post 500* (Summer 1986) plus various issues.

International Monetary Fund. *International Financial Statistics: Yearbook* (IMF Annual, various years).

Johnson, Harry G. "The Efficiency and Welfare Implications of the International Corporation," in Charles P. Kindleberger, ed., *The International Corporation* (Cambridge, Mass.: MIT Press, 1970): 35–56.

Kemp, Murray C. *The Pure Theory of International Trade* (Englewood Cliffs, N.J.: Prentice-Hall, 1964).

Lane, A. W. A. "Economic Integration—Some Aspects of the European Experience" (Ottawa: Department of External Affairs, 1986).

Lea, Sperry. *A Canadian-U.S. Free Trade Agreement: A Survey of Possible Characteristics.* Washington, D.C.: Canadian-American Committee, 1963.

Lipsey, Richard E. "Fears of Job Losses are Overstated." *The Financial Post* (Jan. 11, 1986): 7.

Litvak, Isaiah A., and Christopher J. Maule. *The Canadian Multinationals* (Toronto: Butterworths, 1981).

MacCharles, Donald C. "Do Foreign-Controlled Subsidiaries Have a Future?." *The Canadian Business Review* (Spring 1984): 18–24.

———. "Trade Investment and Knowledge Flows in Relation to Multinational Enterprises: The Canadian Experience." Discussion Paper 8511 (Ottawa: The Institute for Research on Public Policy, 1985a).

———. "Increased Competition and Canada's Domestic and International Trade Flows." *Canadian Journal of Administrative Studies* 2:2 (Dec. 1985b).

———. *Trade Among Multinational Enterprises: Intra-Industry Trade and National Competitiveness* (London: Croom-Helm, 1987).

McDonald, Duncan. "A Fit Place for Investment?." Study no. 81 (Ottawa: Conference Board of Canada, 1984).

MacDougall, G. D. A. "The Benefits and Costs of Private Investment from Abroad: A Theoretical Analysis." *Economic Record*, 36

(1960): 13–35. Reprinted in the *Bulletin of the Oxford University Institute of Statistics*, 22 (Aug. 1960): 189–211.

McGuiness, Norman M., and H. Allan Conway. "World Product Mandates: The Need for Directed Search Strategies," in Hamid Etemad and Louise Seguin Dulude, eds., *Managing the Multinational Subsidiary* (London and Sydney: Croom Helm, 1986): 736–58.

McNaught, K. *The Pelican History of Canada* (Harmondsworth Eng.: Penguin Books, 1982).

McVey, J. S. *Mergers, Plant Openings and Closings of Large Transnational and Other Enterprises: 1970–1976* (Ottawa: Statistics Canada, Supply and Services Canada, catalogue no. 67–507 occasional, Jan. 1981).

Magee, Stephen P. "Information and the Multinational Corporation: An Appropriability Theory of Direct Foreign Investment," in Jagdish W. Bhagwati, ed., *The New International Economic Order* (Cambridge, Mass.: MIT Press, 1977): 315–340.

Matheson, Neil. *Canadian Investment Abroad* (Montreal: International Business Council of Canada, Apr. 18, 1985).

Mundell, Robert A. "International Trade and Factor Mobility," *American Economic Review* 47 (June 1957): 321–35.

Porter, Michael E. *Competitive Strategy: Techniques for Analyzing Industries and Competitors* (New York: Macmillan, The Free Press, 1980).

———. *Competitive Advantage: Creating and Sustaining Superior Performance* (New York: Macmillan, The Free Press, 1985).

———, ed. *Competition in Global Industries* (Boston, Mass.: Harvard Business School Press, 1986).

Poynter, Thomas A., and Alan M. Rugman. "World Product Mandates: How Will Multinationals Respond?" *Business Quarterly* 47:3 (1982): 54–61.

Reisman, Simon. "Trade Policy Options in Perspective," in David W. Conklin and Thomas J. Courchene, eds., *Canadian Trade at a Crossroads: Options for New International Agreements* (Ontario: Ontario Economic Council Special Research Report, 1985): 385–400.

Rugman, Alan M. *International Diversification and the Multinational Enterprise* (Lexington, Mass. and Toronto: D. C. Heath, 1979).

——— . "A New Theory of the Multinational Enterprise: Internationalization versus Internalization." *The Columbia Journal of World Business* 15:1 (Spring 1980a): 23–29.

——— . *Multinationals in Canada: Theory, Performance and Economic Impact* (Boston: Martinus Nijhoff, 1980b).

——— . *Inside the Multinationals: The Economics of Internal Markets* (New York: Columbia University Press, 1981).

——— . "Multinational Enterprises and World Product Mandates" in Alan M. Rugman, ed., *Multinationals and Technology Transfer* (New York: Praeger, 1983a): 73–80.

——— . "Canada: FIRA Updated." *Journal of World Trade Law*, 17:41 (1983b): 352–55.

——— . "Multinationals and Global Competitive Strategy." *International Studies of Management and Organization* 15:2 (Summer 1985a): 8–18.

——— . "The Determinants of Intra-Industry Direct Foreign Investment," in Asim Erdilek, ed., *Multinationals as Mutual Invaders: Intra-Industry Direct Foreign Investment* (London: Croom Helm, 1985b): 38–59.

——— . *Outward Bound: Canadian Direct Investment in United States* (Toronto: C. D. Howe Institute for the Canadian-American Committee, July 1987).

Rugman, Alan M., and Andrew Anderson. *Administered Protection in America.* (London: Croom Helm; Toronto and New York: Methuen, 1987).

Rugman, Alan M., and Sheila Douglas. "The Strategic Management of Multinationals and World Product Mandating." *Canadian Public Policy* 12:2 (June 1986): 320–28.

Rugman, Alan M., and Lorraine Eden, eds. *Multinationals and Transfer Pricing* (London and New York: Croom Helm and St. Martin's Press, 1985).

Rugman, Alan M., Donald Lecraw, and Laurence Booth. *International Business: Firm and Environment* (New York: McGraw Hill, 1985).

Rugman, Alan M., and John McIlveen. *Megafirms: Strategies for Canada's Multinationals* (Toronto: Methuen, 1985).

——— . "Canadian Foreign Direct Investment in the United States," in Peter Gray, ed., *Uncle Sam as Host: Research in International Business and Finance,* vol. 5 (JAI Press, 1986): 289–307.

Rugman, Alan M., and Mark Warner. "Corporate Responses to Free Trade: Strategies for Canadian Multinationals." *National Centre for Management Research and Development* working paper 88–10, University of Western Ontario, May 1988.

Safarian, A. E. *Foreign Ownership of Canadian Industry* (Toronto: McGraw-Hill of Canada, 1966).

Safarian, A. E. "The Relationship Between Trade Agreements and International Direct Investment," in David W. Conklin and Thomas J. Courchene, eds., *Canadian Trade at a Crossroads: Options for New International Agreements* (Toronto: Ontario Economic Council, 1985): 206–21.

Scott, Bruce R., and George C. Lodge, eds. *U.S. Competitiveness in the World Economy* (Cambridge, Mass.: Harvard Business School Press, 1985).

Stern, Robert M. "Global Dimensions and Determinants of International Trade and Investment in Services," in Robert M. Stern, ed., *Trade and Investment in Services: Canada/U.S. Perspectives* (Toronto: Ontario Economic Council, 1985): 126–68.

Stopford, John. *The World Directory of Multinational Enterprises 1982–83* (London: Macmillan, 1982).

Stopford, John, and John H. Dunning. *Multinationals: Company Performance and Global Trends* (London: Macmillan Publishers Ltd., 1983).

Stuckey, John A. *Verticle Integration and Joint Ventures in the Aluminum Industry* (Cambridge, Mass.: Harvard University Press, 1983).

Teece, David J. "Towards an Economic Theory of the Multiproduct Firm." *Journal of Economic Behavior and Organization* 3 (Mar. 1982): 39–64.

Tharakan, P. K. M. *Intra-Industry Trade: Empirical and Methodological Aspects,* (Amsterdam: North-Holland, 1983).

Touche Ross. "Survey" (New York: Sept. 1986).

Urquhart, M. C., and K. A. M. Buckley, eds. *Historical Statistics of Canada,* (Cambridge: Cambridge University Press, 1965).

U.S. Department of Commerce. Bureau of Economic Analysis. *U.S. Direct Investment Abroad, 1977* (Washington, D.C.: International Investment Division, Apr. 1981).

—————. *Foreign Direct Investment in the United States: Annual Survey Results: Revised 1981 Estimates* (Washington, D.C.: Dec. 1984).

———. *Foreign Direct Investment in the United States: Annual Survey Results: Revised 1982 Estimates* (Washington, D. C.: Dec. 1985a).

———. *Foreign Direct Investment in the United States: Operations of U.S. Affiliates, 1977–80* (Washington, D.C.: 1985b).

———. *U.S. Direct Investment Abroad: 1982 Benchmark Survey Data* (Washington, D.C.: Dec. 1985c).

———. *Foreign Direct Investment in the United States: Annual Survey Results: Revised 1983 Estimates* (Washington, D.C.: Oct. 1986a).

———. *Foreign Direct Investment in the United States: Annual Survey Results: Preliminary 1984 Estimates* (Washington, D.C.: Oct. 1986b).

———. *U.S. Direct Investment Abroad: Operations of U.S. Parent Companies and Their Foreign Affiliates, Preliminary 1984 Estimates* (Washington, D.C.: Oct. 1986c).

———. *U.S. Direct Investment Abroad: Operations of U.S. Parent Companies and Their Foreign Affiliates, Revised 1983 Estimates* (Washington, D.C.: Oct. 1986d).

U.S. Department of Commerce, International Trade Administration. *Foreign Direct Investment in the United States; Completed Transactions, 1974–1983. Volume 1: Source Country* (Washington, D.C.: U.S. Government Printing Office, June 1985).

Vernon, Raymond. "International Investment and International Trade in the Product Cycle." *Quarterly Journal of Economics* 30 (May 1966): 190–207.

Whalley, John. *Canadian Trade Policies and the World Economy* (Toronto: University of Toronto Press, 1985).

Williamson, Oliver E. *Markets and Hierarchies: Analysis and Antitrust Implications* (New York: Macmillan, The Free Press, 1975).

———. "The Modern Corporation: Origins, Evolution, Attributes." *Journal of Economic Literature*, 19 (Dec. 1981): 1537–68.

———. *The Economic Institutions of Capitalism* (New York: Macmillan, The Free Press, 1985).

Wolf, Bernard. "The Reaction of Multinational Enterprises to Sectoral Free Trade Between Canada and the United States" (York University mimeo, 1984).

——— . "Canadian Direct Investment in the United States: The Impact of Freer Trade." Paper to the North American Economics and Finance Association Allied Social Sciences Association meetings Dec. 28–30, 1985.

Wonnacott, Ronald J. "Free Trade Saves Jobs." *Canadian Public Policy* 12:1 (Mar. 1986): 258–63.

Name Index

Company Index